THE ART

of

FEMININE

Seduction

THE ART
of
FEMININE
Seduction

ALANA MCKENZIE PAGE

QUANTUM SHIFT
PUBLISHING

For information about special discounts for bulk purchases, please contact hello@sovereign-dating.com

Editing, cover, and interior design by Quantum Shift Media

978-1-955533-12-6 Paperback
978-1-955533-13-3 eBook

Library of Congress Control Number: 2023900539

Printed in the United States

QUANTUM SHIFT
PUBLISHING

Denver, Colorado

DEDICATION

For my husband – my favorite date!

PREFACE

During my teen years, I was romantically overlooked. I was one of two girls in my high school class who did not get asked to senior prom by an obliging classmate.

I went on to date men I hadn't agreed to date, men who were in love with other women, or men who were with other women and lying to both of us. I went through a phase in college where I dated guys who were friends of friends, thinking that it would solve my so-called aversion to nice guys.

After college, my work led me to travel abroad, so I dated on three different continents. Surely, I reasoned, there was a great man *somewhere* on earth who would find me appealing. Instead, I was strung along, left, lied to, emotionally abused, and ghosted in five different languages.

I wanted a huge romance with passion and fun, and commitment.

But my experience with men was always that a) they didn't really try to get to know me, b) they didn't want to spend much time with me, or c) they weren't ready for any kind of commitment.

I wasn't someone men wanted.

Years of building up hope and being disappointed by love interests left me discouraged. It began to feel like I was waiting for the next wrong man to show up and fail me. I waited and wished for the magical day when my dream partner would finally arrive and love me fully and totally for who I am.

It felt like everyone around me was capable of finding someone to commit to them. For years, I watched as friends and acquaintances got into relationships, left relationships and found new relationships, and sometimes created serious relationships. Several of my friends got married and started families of their own. Yet, I remained consistently single, feeling left out and left behind in love.

Honestly, I worried I might be an unlovable freak.

And then, by some twist of fate, I discovered the science and spiritual art behind creating relationships. And I transformed the way dating went for me.

At the time of my discovery, I was living in Bucharest. I was casually seeing Constantin, a long-lashed, strong-jawed Romanian. He was tall, attractive, intelligent, and kind. When I say we were casually seeing each other, I mean he would say things like, "let's hang out Sunday," and I would reply, "Yes, please!" and then he would cease to communicate with me for another week and a half. By that time in my dating history, I was used to being treated that way and did not protest. What differentiated Constantin from other men I had dated was that he refused to sleep with me. His refusal contradicted my usual dating belief that men only wanted to date me for sex, so I was partially intrigued by his denial of sexual contact with me.

Unfortunately, I interpreted his avoidance of sex as further confirmation that I was undesirable. I took it to mean that I was so undesirable that even a man dating me had to use non-religious reasons to avoid sleeping with me. We would take steamy showers together and make out in bed, and then he would say goodnight and turn over to sleep. I was cast into a world of insecurity and doubt: was he gay or asexual, or did he just not like me very much?

He would call me on the phone and talk about culture and philosophy for hours. He took me on sexy spa dates where we would soak half-naked in mineral pools. We sweat in 11 different saunas while attendants splashed us with ice water or offered us diffused aromatherapeutic oils to inhale. We smeared exfoliating mud on each other's bodies. After these sensual dates, he would drop me off at my home nonchalantly as bedtime came around rather than suggesting we spend the night together.

"Thank you for tonight," I would say graciously, "that was wonderful."

And then, I would close the car door and turn towards my apartment building door alone, feeling utterly lost, confused, and helpless. I was already certain I was unwanted and incompetent at love, so his actions affirmed that belief. I did not have insight into how my own actions created a lack of intimacy and connection between us. I never asked him why he wouldn't sleep with me or invite him in to my apartment.

But no matter how disappointing it was to date him, I didn't want to date anyone else. I was so tired of trying and failing to find the kind of love I wanted. I was tired of the fact that dating only led to heartbreak, the small ones, and the large ones, sending me on emotional roller coasters that left me drained and sometimes dysfunctional in other areas of life. I settled for his inconsistent companionship and non-committal attention because at least I knew to expect nothing from him. I had surrendered fully to the idea that the kind of love I craved was either non-existent or not meant for me.

Around four months into this kind of half-hearted dating, we made dinner at his place, and he suggested we shower together. I knew this meant caressing each other's naked bodies with soap and making out under hot water. It was late, so I knew he wouldn't want to drive me home after, and I would be spending the night. Perhaps it would be the night he finally wanted me enough to sleep with me.

I went to the bathroom and began undressing. He did not join me. I finished undressing and turned on the water, adjusting the tap to the perfect heat and allowing the water to fall freely from the shower head. He was not yet there, but I stepped into the bathtub. I stood naked at the dry end of the tub, observing Constantin's movements through the open bathroom door. He was still down the hall, straightening up the living room. Several minutes ago, he had suggested this shower, but it seemed his plan had shifted to prioritize cleanliness. He picked up glasses and bowls from our meal and took them into the kitchen. He washed the dishes, dried them, and put them away.

I stood there with the water running, by myself, soapless, watching and waiting. Thoughts were flying through my mind. *I'm dating a man who would rather wash dishes than be naked in the shower with me. I come second on the priority list to dishes. Men never say no to a naked woman. What is it about me that I can end up with a man who doesn't even want me for my body?*

Fifteen minutes later, when the living room was fully in order, the kitchen scrubbed, and the cups dried and put away, he entered the bathroom. He took off his clothes and joined me in the shower, ready to wash me with the same tenderness I believe the dishes received. Afterward, I sat on the edge of his bed wearing one of his T-Shirts, quiet and pensive as he got ready for sleep. I was already heading into the familiar territory of the shutdown I experienced when dating was going poorly. When we were both settled in bed, I mustered up enough bravery to ask a direct question.

"So, you don't want to have sex?" I inquired, the words feeling coarse and awkward as I spoke them out into the world.

"I'm practicing an ancient Tibetan technique of no sex," he replied.

"Oh," I said, "Cool."

And that was that. He offered no further explanation, and I was too confused by his answer to ask further questions.

As he fell asleep, I lay awake pondering my dating history. The boys who never wanted me. The men who disappeared and reappeared in my life. Willing to play with me. Unwilling to take me seriously. Wanting me, but never all of me.

Finally, feeling alone, lying right next to him, I drifted off to sleep.

At home the next day, I decided to look into that ancient Tibetan technique Constantin was practicing. I googled "ancient Tibetan sexual techniques." What was he working on? What benefits would it give him? What was he trying to achieve? There was no immediately clear answer to my query. There were many Tibetan sexual techniques, ranging from energy work to breathing techniques and a host of philosophical teachings. I was fascinated but could not find any mention of a technique where sex was avoided, except in cases of monastic celibacy. I kept digging. Surely, some corner of the Internet would mention the technique. As I searched, I came across other dating techniques and relationship research. I found therapists and coaches who helped people overcome a plethora of romantic issues. There were countless programs, books, and articles, all devoted to helping people just like me who were struggling to find the love they wanted to experience.

Over many months, I went down, down, down a rabbit hole of ancient Tibetan philosophy, tantra, energy work, and scientific dating and mating research. It became the single focus of my non-working hours. I watched Ted Talks and YouTube videos over dinner and read books and articles by relationship experts and marriage psychologists while traveling to work on the metro. I consumed information about dating psychology and the neurology of attraction and sexual arousal before bed. I devoted every weekend Constantin suggested that we see each other, and then disappeared to the study of dating.

I watched reality TV shows about first dates and new relationships to observe what I was learning in action. The research and the stories on-screen brought me face to face with all the mistakes I had made with men over the years. Acknowledging my mistakes presented me with new ways to approach dating and relationships. I began to see how I had silenced my voice, asked for less than I desired, and tried to please men to keep them around. Unfortunately, I had tried to please men without first understanding what they wanted. And I had made my own desire less important than theirs. Over and over again, I had kept what I wanted secret in order to avoid being hurt, and ironically ended up hurt every time.

I had dated passively, waiting for a man to prove himself to me without giving him directions on what to prove. I had not allowed men to make me happy, and I ended up dissatisfied in love. I had disbelieved I was worthy of the love I wanted. I spent more time worrying about whether I was attractive enough for the person I was dating than getting to know who they were and what they wanted. I had subconsciously been waiting for someone to show me I was worthy of the love I wanted instead of claiming it for myself and not settling for less. With one exception, I had avoided true intimacy in every connection. I had failed to ask important questions. I had poor boundaries and weird energy around attraction. I had believed that love would simply happen for me as I assumed it happened for others.

By acknowledging my mistakes and integrating the new information available to me, I began to transform my thoughts about dating. Outside of Buddhist monk culture and complete devotion to celibacy, I never found mention of any ancient Tibetan techniques that required men to abstain from sex. Likely, Constantin made that up, and I did not bother to ask him more about it. Although there was a high level of intellectual intimacy in our relationship, and we could always share high-brow ideas, there was no deep emotional intimacy and trust. I did not trust him with my feelings, and I spent a lot of energy tiptoeing around what I perceived his feelings to be. I didn't try to apply what I was learning with him; I was just absorbing information in the background.

As the months passed and I studied dating, nothing much changed in our relationship. We were both committed to our non-commitment to each other. We had game nights with groups of his friends, went to festivals together, and had deep phone conversations. Looking back, it is astounding how little emotional intimacy we managed to create after spending so much time together. Time does not equal intimacy. He was consistently inconsistent, and I was consistently passive about his behavior and feelings. I made no fuss when he disappeared for days on end and never asked him for time, sex, or commitment. I was unaware that I held half the power in the relationship. I was always waiting for him to decide what he wanted, to make a move, and to ask me for more.

And then, with less than a month left on my graduate school student visa, the company I was working for admitted that they had not started the work visa process that would allow me to stay in the country. They suggested that I extend my student visa. I spent a week running around to different school offices and government agencies looking for a visa solution. That's when I learned you could not extend a student visa after the program has ended. University classes were already well underway, so applying for another degree was out of the question. Sponsoring my visa through my own business would cost me at least €600 per month, twice the cost of my apartment rent. Ultimately, I couldn't find a viable solution or a reason to stay. I realized I was tired of Romanian bureaucracy, tired of working as a corporate trainer, and tired of trying to make my Romanian life work in general. I was ready to move on.

In 15 days, I needed to leave the country, collapsing the life I had built over several years in Romania. My cozy apartment, successful corporate training and language tutoring business, cat ownership, plans with local friends, and my undefined relationship with Constantin would all come to their unique ends.

Constantin was away at a mountain hiking retreat, and he had told me he would have unreliable service while there. Although I saw him appear on Facebook many times, he didn't contact me all week or the week after he came home. I decided not to bother him with news of my impending departure. I could already taste the bitterness of neglect, and my automatic response was always: *Fine. You obviously don't need or care about me anyway. I don't need you.* After all, I had plenty to do, thanks to sorting and packing up my business, home, and emotions.

Once I decided to leave Romania for good, my next move fell right into place. A friend invited me to stay with her in Istanbul while I planned the next phase of my life. I had been there the year before and fallen in love with the city, so it was an easy yes. A Romanian friend took my beautiful orange tabby, James. My landlord said my departure was perfectly timed because he wanted to renovate the apartment. I was ending an intense work contract in my business. Everything about my life in Romania wrapped up quickly and efficiently.

A week before I left, Constantin finally called. My unimportance to him seemed validated by the fact that I had changed my entire life since he had last reached out to me. I gave him the news of my departure passively.

"What? No!" He exclaimed, "what can we do?"

"I've tried everything," I said, "I leave next week."

"Let me make some calls," he said, taking charge.

"Okay," I agreed, and we hung up.

But his attempts to solve my visa issue hit the same walls mine had. There wasn't anything to do. We said our goodbyes and I gifted him some of my favorite philosophy books for good measure. I had never allowed myself to fall in love with him, but I did think he was wonderful. I packed up my apartment into three large suitcases, stored some of my belongings with a friend, and boarded a plane for Turkey.

I felt blown by the wind, unsure of what to do next with my life, and totally exhausted from my last month in Romania. I spent my first few weeks resting in the limbo of a lost life and the pure potential of my next chapter. I walked along the shores of the sea of Marmara and felt life force coming back into me. I began to remember a time when I was less apathetic about my life. I could do anything; what would I possibly choose? I decided to try dating again, only this time, I would do it differently. I was no longer going to try to find *The One*. I was simply going to practice the dating and intimacy-building techniques I had learned. I got on a dating app and began the work of finding matches in Istanbul. I applied what I had learned about dating psychology and feminine energy in the last months in Romania. Like a good dating scientist, I had to see for myself whether this energy thing had any validity. Immediately, dating went differently for me. In the very first month I used feminine energy, I found a dating connection with a man that was everything I had ever dreamed of - sexy, intimate, fresh, and interesting, yet not obsessive on my end.

As it went, I didn't stay in Turkey long-term. My next chapter took me all around the world again, allowing me to date multiple men from various cultures. Using the teaching in this book, I shifted into a completely new dating paradigm. I raised my feminine sexual energy higher and higher and attracted greater numbers of men while also experiencing more profound connections with them. I met interesting and sexy men who wanted and pursued me over and over again. It was a revelation. Without changing who I was, I became desirable. Men flirted with me, asked me out, called me back, and wrote to me after I had left their countries. Men treated me like I was precious, bought things for me, traveled to see me, and asked me for commitment. Thus, the journey of feminine seduction began for me. For the first time in my life, love and romance became fun rather than stressful or heartbreaking. I became someone who knew how to get what I wanted in love.

At a point in the middle of my journey, I thought, *why doesn't everyone know this?!* So many women I spoke to felt down about how their love lives were going or not going. So many women had disempowering hang-ups about dating and sex. I wanted everyone to know it doesn't have to be this way. I created a business to empower women to show up differently in relationships. I used my background in teaching to create a curriculum that taught women to access power in dating, sex, and love. I began teaching women to experience the same transformation I did, to master the art of feminine seduction. This book is that curriculum in written form. If a new dating paradigm is what you seek, you have come to the right place.

ACKNOWLEDGMENTS

I always imagined that writing a book meant huddling over a typewriter in a quaint, ivy-strewn cottage alone. In fact, writing a book was a highly social endeavor for me. This book would not exist without the support of the large community of people mentioned on these pages.

First, my eternal thanks to every woman who said yes to working on their seductive energy in my live program. Your stories and demonstrations of strength, grace, and perseverance in the face of dating pain clarified this work for me and inspired me to keep writing.

Second, to all the men in this book who were loves or lessons. Meeting you led me to some of my life's most significant realizations and work. I am decidedly grateful to each and every one of you. To all the men I didn't write in, you matter, too.

A huge shout out to my top Indiegogo contributors who helped me take the leap to get published. Sergey Kochergan, Corrine Porter, Sandra Weber, Jessica Decker, Ornella Manera, Joseph Page, John McKenzie, and Aidan McKenzie, I am so grateful for both your monetary support and your belief in my book.

To my writing community at Quantum Shift Publishing, Alicia Ehr Martinez, Daniel A. Linder, Karen Krueger, Jodi Scholes, Lara Buelow, and Diana Proemm, thank you for holding the collective writing space and for your insights into authorship.

My heartfelt thanks to life coaches Jen Westra of *Life On Purpose Coaching* and Linda Scholten (who writes historical fiction) of *Touchstone Coaching*. Your support was invaluable to me on this journey, and the coworking sessions you hosted got me through my stickiest author moments.

I also want to thank my Natural Success coaching group, Harpreet Sandhu, Katja Steinbach, Jennifer Groff, Rachel Ellis Bloch, Anna Schoonhoven, Carmen Iordache, Isabel Pereza, and Janet Amateau. Your encouragement and reality checks helped me remember my power to choose my book at every turn.

I am incredibly grateful to my brilliant reading buddy, Amy Palatnick. Your feedback and excitement about my writing buoyed me, and your example of vulnerability in your dating book, *Can I Be Honest With You?* played a major role in my sharing so openly in this book.

Special thanks to my photographers Kenji Mizumori, Irene Elena Rose, and Scott Lipner, who helped bring my book brand to life through imagery.

To my dexterous editor, Abigail Batton, a resounding thank you for shaping and honing this book into a more understandable, cohesive, and interesting body of work.

My infinite, undying gratitude to Keren Kilgore of Quantum Shift Media. This book was possible due to your author's guidance, publishing program, edits, designs, and knowledge. Your support at every stage of the writing and publishing process meant the world to me, helped me keep going, and contributed indispensably to my confidence that I wasn't constantly off-track.

And lastly, to my husband, my best friend, and my big love story, thank you for all that you do, for how you love, and for giving me a playground to live the art of feminine seduction every day.

TABLE OF CONTENTS

INTRODUCTION

You can have what you want in love.

It doesn't matter ...

...how many times you've failed to find love.

...if dating is fun for three months but never longer.

...if you haven't even met one single real romantic potential.

It doesn't even matter what you look like or where you come from.

You can become the woman your dates call back right away.

You can become the woman they can't stop thinking about.

You can become the woman they want to see over and over again.

You can become the one they ask for commitment.

Regardless of your personal dating history, a sexually *and* emotionally desired woman is inside you. Even if your current dating reality leads to you watching mind-numbing hours of TV and eating an entire box of chocolate alone while persistently telling yourself you are too ugly, fat, and worthless to be loved.

I have been there. On my lowest days, I told myself, *even serial killers on death row get more serious attention from lovers than I do as a free woman in the dating pool.*

But then, through learning what I'm teaching in this book, I transformed into a woman who men found fascinating. I became a woman who men traveled to see. Men bought me gifts and wanted to commit to me without prodding. Quite quickly, after applying the principles found in this book, I began to experience romantic attention and sexual fulfillment in a whole new and pleasurable way. I did not have to change who I was or what I look like. There was no magic movie moment where the right dress, makeup and taking off my glasses turned me into a femme fatale. Instead, I underwent a much more subtle and powerful shift.

The shift was a transformation of energy.

The energy I refer to is the personal energetic frequency you put out into the world. On one level, your personal energy rules aspects of your life that other people easily read. These include your energy level, body language, tone of voice, and general communication style. On another level, your energetic state is less visible but highly potent. Inside of you is an energetic essence. Have you ever noticed that some people command respect while others tend to be the butt of the joke? Have you noticed that some people seem to have fulfilling relationships effortlessly drop into their lap while others can't seem to find love despite years of trying?

The difference between these groups is their energy and, specifically, very subtle differences in their energetic presence. These subtleties elicit a response from those around them. By reclaiming and shifting your energy, you can transform your essence. You can become a woman who is wanted.

The name of the energy you will transform is feminine sexual energy, as defined by various ancient cultures and spiritual traditions. When I first discovered this teaching, the term *feminine energy* made me cringe a bit. At the time, I was not into *woo-woo* and was distrustful of anything too far outside the bounds of modern science. Despite having personal experiences with Tibetan meditation and receiving messages in nature that science could not explain, I was uncomfortable with believing there was more to life than meets the eye or microscope. I did not relish terms like *energies*, *manifesting*, or *soulmate*.

But I really wanted a freaking hot boyfriend who was nice to me, and I was so desperate to change my dating results I was willing to try feminine energy. Nothing else had worked, so I figured I might as well give it a try. And boy, did it work.

On the most basic, oversimplified level, feminine energy is internal, whereas masculine energy is externally based. The energetic principles relate to how males and females experience their roles in human reproduction. The female contribution to human procreation occurs inside the body, receiving the sperm and growing the baby, while the male offering is the outwardly directed ejaculation. In the same vein, feminine energy is what you experience when you focus on your inner state. Masculine energy is the energy you put out into the world when you talk, act, or affect change outside of yourself. You spend time turned inward in your feminine energy, daydreaming, noticing a pang of hunger in your body, or sleeping. You spend as much or more time in masculine action, moving around, engaging with others, and speaking, writing, or drawing your thoughts into the outside world. To be clear, everyone has both feminine and masculine energy.

There is one caveat to the statement that everyone has both feminine and masculine energy. Generally, people feel more naturally attuned to either feminine or masculine energy when connecting with a potential sexual partner. You will likely identify as leaning more feminine or masculine energetically while searching for a mate. If you lean feminine, you have core feminine sexual energy.

How do you know if you have core feminine sexual energy? Like your sexual preference, you just *know*. You may have always disassociated with the identity around the word feminine but feel more comfortable living in the energetic states outlined in this book. You will find out by reading further. One hint: if you are estrogen-predominant, you likely have core feminine energy.

I wrote this book for women who are seeking committed relationships with men. I am a white, able-bodied, cis-gendered, heterosexual woman who dated to find a monogamous marriage and create a family. Those labels don't need to describe you to the tee for you to be able to get what you want in love using the energetic states in this book. They are simply the lens through which I experienced dating and conducted my research, so I want to acknowledge the bias in these pages. This book is not intended as a reflection of the full meaning of feminine nor a statement about what kinds of relationship are desirable. I can't personally speak to the energetics of polyamorous or LGBTQI+ dating because I haven't experienced them, nor conducted thorough research. If you perform that research, please reach out anytime; I would love to hear about your experience and findings.

Learning the Art of Feminine Seduction

This book will teach you everything you need to know about the art of feminine seduction. You will discover seven specific energy shifts that will give you the power to choose your energetic state while dating, make you attractive, and help you connect with sexy, potential lovers. You will learn the seven feminine energy shifts in chapters four to ten. Applying them in dating gives you a sexy glow, an intriguing presence, and a powerful ability to connect. You will learn how to turn your feminine energy up or down at a whim. Here are those shifts:

1. From masculine doing to feminine being
2. From masculine giving to feminine receiving
3. From masculine mental to feminine physical
4. From masculine structure to feminine wild
5. From masculine logistics to feminine emotion
6. From masculine timelines to feminine timelessness
7. From masculine initiation to feminine process

These energies will help you become someone whose sexual power is clear and embodied. You will feel confident being yourself in dating. Each of the shifts correlates to dating psychology and behavior that creates healthy, sustainable, sexually and emotionally fulfilling relationships. Combined, they will help you transform your dating experience and create a love beyond your wildest dreams.

Three-Ingredient Process

Besides the seven energy shifts, you will also learn a three-ingredient process for what I call *The Seduction Phase* of a relationship. The Seduction Phase is the special time in a relationship when you create a bond of a romantic or sexual nature. It is usually when you first start dating, but it can also apply to relationships that have been friendships and are now transitioning into romance or even long-term relationships that have lost their spark but are being revived. To forge a sexy, romantic relationship that is also meaningful and likely to last past a few sexual encounters, you must bring all three of these ingredients to the connection:

1. Attraction
2. Sexual Tension
3. Emotional Connection

These three ingredients make up the physiological soup of love - when mixed together, the outcome of their chemistry is seduction. You will discover what these ingredients are and how to create them in dating. Creating these love ingredients with another person entails creating them inside yourself, and the most direct and powerful way to access them is through your energy and focus.

Is Feminine Seduction a Trigger?

Does the term "feminine seduction" make you feel uncomfortable? Congratulations! You've just found an essential area of exploration. The words *feminine* and *seduction* have a charge for people for a variety of reasons. Initially, both of them triggered me.

Now the trigger in the words *feminine* and *seduction* is precisely why I like them. They hold power, history, and deep, sometimes unconscious, meaning for people. Working with these words and their triggers invites you to transform from first contact. The word *feminine* can help you recognize and heal parts of yourself you have abandoned, suppressed, or verbally abused. The word *seduction* can help you rewrite your relationship to your sexual power. As you read this book, I encourage you to explore your relationship to these words.

The Trigger of Feminine

Much of my personal charge around the word *feminine* came from my fear of being boxed in as a woman. I had deeply internalized that to be feminine meant to be a certain kind of woman. I believed that feminine meant "wears pink, likes dresses, gets pedicures, is soft, quiet, and graceful." And to be sure, I genuinely love manicures and luxurious clothing, and I prefer to be graceful rather than clumsy. I wanted to do and be this version of feminine, but I also wanted to be more than that. In fact, I *am* more than that. Often, I am loud, I hustle, and I am exuberant in action and words. I enjoy heated intellectual debates. Sometimes I am very direct instead of soft and polite. I exaggerate too much, a man I liked once pointed out to me as a flaw that made me undesirable. Possessing these traits deemed culturally *un-feminine* made me feel that *feminine* was a test of womanhood that I would never pass. I chose to disassociate from the word rather than examine my inherited judgments against its meaning.

I was triggered because I was associating feminine with an identity, rather than energy. I believed feminine was another box I either fit into or didn't, rather than an energetic state I could visit or shed at will. If you feel triggered by the word *feminine*, quickly check in with yourself if you associate feminine with an identity or personality trait.

Feminine, in this book, refers to the energetic feminine based on ancient spiritual traditions and archetypes. It refers to an energy rather than a personality, identity, gender, or sex. Embodying feminine energy is not about becoming more of a *woman*. You do not need to be female to work with feminine energy. You experience your feminine energy when you focus on your inner state, which is energy any self-aware person can focus on. In our discussion, feminine is an energy, not an identity.

The Trigger of Seduction

I find that the term *seduction* is objectionable to those who feel discomfort around their own sexual power. I certainly used to feel this way, and many clients and students have come up against discomfort with the word seduction. It is common for women and feminine energy folks to feel disempowered around their sexual expression.

My early female learning and experience taught me that it was better and safer to suppress, downplay, and act without my sexual nature. Overtly sexual women were considered desperate, slutty, and suffering from daddy issues. Being a sexual woman could get you demonized and ostracized from respectable groups. I learned that being a sexual woman was about performing for men rather than expressing something powerful about the female nature. I did not want to be this kind of woman. I created an entire persona around the suppression of my sexual nature. The avoidance of my sexual power manifested as giving little to no hints that I was an innately sexual being, from how I carried myself to my expressions, actions, and dress. I clothed myself with others in mind, careful to hide my sexuality or play it up appropriately for the situation rather than wear what would make me happy. I made decisions from the outside in, always careful to first consider how others would view me rather than what gave me pleasure.

I was unaware of how living this way created negative self-consciousness. I spent a lot of energy overthinking and doubting my actions and words, often choosing not to express them. In dating, I showed up with little or no emotion. I waited for permission to love and be loved. I led with my intellect in all social situations, including romance, believing, and simultaneously seeking to prove to others that my brain was the most valuable part of me, rather than my innate or sexual nature.

This is just me being me, I even told myself. *I'm just not a very sexual person.* But in reality, I had bottled up my sexual nature because I felt it was more acceptable to others if I hid it away. And then, deep down, more than anything, I wanted someone incredible and irresistible to fall in love with me totally and completely. I wanted to be desired. I wanted to seduce and be seduced, but I was unwilling to admit it.

Sometimes, people object to the word *seduction* because they associate it with manipulation. You cannot manipulate with feminine energy, because, by definition, it is focused inward on your own self. Becoming energetically seductive is about learning to change *your* energy, which in turn changes other people's energy. Not because you forced or manipulated their energy to change somehow, but because you showed up in your energetic sovereignty. Once you have sovereignty over your own sexual energy, you will find you are less worried about whether you can get someone to like you, want you, call you back, or commit to you. Ironically, it's these worries which usually lead to actual controlling and manipulative behavior in dating. I believe I carried out more underhanded, sneaky, and dishonest dating behavior before feminine seduction became part of my life. I did not know what I wanted, if I was worth what I wanted, or how to get what I wanted. My dating energy was wishy-washy and misleading. I tried lots of weird dating tactics and told lots of white lies. Claiming my power to seduce on my own terms changed that.

Sometimes, people unconsciously feel discomfort about the term seduction because of its close relationship to sexual desire. Sexual desire can feel like a dark and dangerous place, with shame and confusion wrapped around it. It is no wonder a word like *seduction* brings up strange body sensations and negative thoughts in many people. If you're feeling uncomfortable with the word right now, notice the discomfort and allow those feelings to hang out with you as you read. Allow the discomfort; no need to force your emotions to change.

In this book, *seduction* refers to the phase of a relationship when you attract someone romantically and sexually using the three ingredients, attraction, sexual tension, and emotional connection. You will learn how to use the three ingredients to become energetically seductive. Becoming energetically seductive is about reclaiming your own sexual power in dating, sex, and love, not about learning to control others.

CHAPTER 1

DESIRE

I once believed that attractiveness was something you either had or didn't. I also thought it depended on your physical appearance. Come to find out; I was wrong in both cases. Attraction goes way beyond physical beauty, and you have the power to attract romance no matter what you look like or how many dead-ends you've reached in dating. No matter who you are, you can become attractive. This book will show you how.

Attractive

Growing up, I was certain I was ugly. As a small child, I had been cute with curly blonde hair and a button nose, which suddenly, at age 11, turned into a frizzy brown mess and a large, awkward appendage off my small face. I no longer received affirmations that I was cute. I did receive a lot of the opposite: advice about how I could fix my appearance. I was not counted as one of the *hot* girls. Once, a man looked straight into my eyes and said matter-of-factly, "well, you know, you're not *that* attractive."

I knew. I knew so much more than he did about how I didn't measure up to other women. By my own perception, I was rarely on par with most women in the room, let alone magazine images of beautiful female entertainers or models. As I grew in age, size, and awareness, I began to add reasons to the list of how I was unattractive. My thighs were too big. My face was too round, my chin too small. My upper arms were too flabby. My conversational skills were lacking, and my "coolness" level was wanting. I received no romantic attention throughout my school years - confirming my shortcomings in beauty and desirability. While other girls got their first kisses and boyfriends, I got more convinced I was unwanted. By 18 years old, I had accepted that I was not a catch. *Hopefully*, I thought, *someone will want me for my personality.* And then my personality failed to attract love for the next decade.

Personality and beauty are not, it turns out, what determine whether people fall in love with you. If beauty were the key, people who identify as beautiful would have no problem finding love. Hollywood relationships would be overwhelmingly successful. If a great personality were the key, people who identify as fun or successful would always be in loving relationships. While being physically beautiful may help you attract attention, it may not be the kind of attention you seek. You may also find that people create fantasies around loving you rather than loving you truly and deeply. While being fun and engaging may help you develop friendships and more excitement in sexual relationships, it doesn't determine whether you will have a successful romantic relationship. You can be fun and still jump from casual relationship to casual relationship without experiencing the love you really want.

Like me, you may believe that the reason you don't have love is the result of your appearance or your personality. But this isn't the case. You do not need to change your looks or personality. After 15 years of experiencing what I didn't want in dating, I discovered the teaching of feminine energy. With nothing left to lose, I began to reclaim my feminine sexual power in the form of my energy. I applied the energetic dating technique in this book and watched my love life recalibrate with astonishing speed.

I became a woman who was wanted by men I wanted. I became a woman men sought out. A woman who men enjoyed talking to and writing to even when sex wasn't directly on the table. I became a woman who felt beautiful, desirable, and lovable. I learned that I had the power to create love whenever I wanted it. Unlocking this power did not require changing my looks or personality. It required changing my energy. Because of how long and hard I struggled with love, I know you can shift your own energy and overcome whatever is holding you back.

The seven shifts that will switch on your attractiveness high beam are being, receiving, physicality, wildness, emotion, timelessness, and process. Through shifting your energy, desirability will begin to creep onto your face and into the rhythm of your walk. You will start to experience the magic of being wanted. When you know for yourself and embody your own desirability, others can't help but feel attracted to you. Practicing the seven energetic shifts in dating will turn you into what I call a great seductress.

A great seductress is someone who is energetically attractive. She is able to create a great romantic relationship whenever she wants. She knows she is desirable, and she knows what she desires. She knows how to get what she wants in love. You can learn all the energy techniques and relationship skills necessary to become a great seductress, and all will be revealed in the following pages. Even if you have never been noticed, never been kissed, or never been loved, you can become an alluring, unforgettable enchantress. You are seven energy shifts away from a high attraction state.

Great Seductress Myth-Busting

I grew up believing in the myth that a great seductress is a gorgeous woman who tempts everyone with her great beauty, and charms them with her quick wit, headstrong confidence, sensual movement, or perhaps a dangerous siren song. These are seductive qualities for sure; however, there are billions of ways to be a great seductress, just as there are billions of different love stories in the world. Your flavor of seduction will be your own. There is no need to fundamentally change who you are. Your own unique humor, introversion, extroversion, intelligence, sense of joy, sadness, fun, and desire will all add to you being the great seductress you are. What's more, you being exactly as you are will naturally attract someone who is a great match for you.

For many years, I remained convinced I had no luck in love because I didn't match society's picture of what a lovable woman looks like. I was caught in the thought trap: because I am not sexy, I cannot be attractive. However, now that I work with women on becoming irresistible, I have met highly seductive women with bent backs and loud laughs and others with genuinely soft, quiet alluring natures. A Hollywood example like Marilyn Monroe may flash across your mind when you think of the perfect seductress, but great seductresses throughout history have had their own unique looks, personalities, and lives.

Humans have been sexually attracted to all kinds of bodies and faces since the dawn of humanity. That's literally how your genes arrived here and now. The myth that you need to look a certain way to be attractive particularly affects women. I truly believed, at one point, that if my nose had been smaller and straighter and if my legs had been slightly longer and leaner, I would have been lovable. I would have received more romantic attention from better men, and therefore I would have had a relationship. That was my logic based on the myth that a particular appearance leads to more romantic attention and sexual success.

Let's explore the legacy of Anais Nin. Nin is known for her passionate and prolific love affairs (she was also married twice), which she recorded in her private diaries. They were eventually published and made very public. You can find pictures of her online. She does not have a classic Hollywood face, but a sharpness in her gaze and openness shines out of her in unmistakable beauty - she knows she is an attractive and alluring woman. Her seductive nature was intelligent and erotic.

Cleopatra, a great queen of ancient Egypt, is known for having been one of few recorded female leaders of antiquity, and for keeping other powerful leaders as lovers, including Julius Caesar and his general, Mark Antony. Although modern films cast her as a delicate-looking beauty, ancient sculptures and portraits portray someone with a strong brow and a very prominent nose. Her beauty is unique, and, combined with her sense of personal power, it turns her into an intriguing, and we can imagine, irresistible wielder of sexual power. In tantric traditions, sexual power is considered a life force. We must imagine she was a life force to be reckoned with and that her seductive allure was powerful enough to convince two foreign military men to choose her over each other.

Catherine the Great, empress of Russia, was a large woman in stature and personality. She was not known for being a great beauty, but she was known to take a considerable number of lovers. In paintings, her eyes are mysterious and portray great strength. She ran an empire during a time when most women were considered the property of a man. Instead of accepting the political status of sovereign breeder, she came to direct political power after overthrowing her Emperor husband. She knew what she wanted and got what she wanted, legislatively and likely also sexually. Her seductive nature was self-sovereignty and royal power. The next time you're tempted to think you don't deserve what you want because of your appearance, remember Catherine and nip that thought in the bud. Attraction is not straightforward.

I often hear from clients, "If only I were younger, had better hair, better skin, lost that last 10 pounds, then it would be easy to find love." Your body is not what determines how seductive you are. Your face doesn't dictate how much healthy romantic attention you receive. Your personality and appearance do not determine your seductiveness. Your energy does. Becoming seductive is not about changing yourself into the caricature of a Hollywood seductress. You do not need to lose weight, color your hair, buy new clothes, learn to walk in high heels, wear a thong, or alter your personality. Attractiveness and seductiveness are energies, and they are ones you can tune into and tune out of when you don't feel like attracting romantic or sexual attention.

The Power of Being Wanted

As a young person, I desperately wanted to find the guy who would fall for me and affirm that I was lovable. I imagined he would pursue me the way men chase women in rom-coms and pop culture - passionately, with lovesick confessions and dramatic acts where he proved his love and devotion. I imagined he would do anything to be with me. I looked for him on public buses, at summer camps, track meets, and at parties. He did not appear to sweep me off my feet. Instead, I graduated high school and moved to Europe, where I began to look for him in bars, pubs, clubs, city streets, and new jobs. *Everyone finds love*, I thought, *everyone has stories of their first love and ex-boyfriends. Mine has to be out there.* I wanted to be wanted.

I met Alec at a billiards table in a London pub, drinking. It was a Thursday. He invited my friends and me to play a game, and we hit it off immediately. We argued passionately and playfully about the rules of American pool versus British snooker, both of which can be played on a billiards table. I had never held the full attention of a male peer for so long nor experienced the feeling of knowing - really knowing - that someone wanted me. I was completely high on life between the male attention and the vodka sodas. When he found out I had never been clubbing, he insisted we go out the following weekend. I accepted the invitation.

When I showed up ready for the club, I discovered I was alone with him. His friends hadn't come out this time. He told me we would grab dinner before the club. I stood there and thought, *I am on my first date.* I was so sure of my undate-ability, that I hadn't even realized I'd been asked on a date. I hadn't understood that I'd agreed to a date.

"I didn't realize this was a date," I told him.

"My bad," he chuckled.

We had a good laugh and continued on toward the restaurant. We ate a fried chicken dinner and headed to a bar for drinks before the club.

On our after-dinner walk, he stopped the conversation in the middle of a blocked-off street, turned toward me, and kissed me slowly and smoothly. His lips were cold. I felt my attention drop to my feet on the concrete and heard London traffic whizzing by in the background.

"Not bad for a first kiss," he said sweetly, pulling back.

"Mmm," I responded noncommittally, while my mind tried to work out what had just happened.

I had just had my first kiss.

And I was terribly confused.

My experience of the kiss was his cold lips and the lack of warmth in my body. I didn't feel any of the fireworks people talked about, nor the desire to experience kissing again. I was actually put off by the gesture. When we arrived at the bar, I went directly to the bathroom. I stared at myself in the mirror and thought, *I have been kissed. I just kissed someone.* I had been imagining that first kiss moment in my mind for years. Was that what it was supposed to be like? Had everyone been blowing this kissing business way out of proportion? Why didn't I feel all the heat and excitement people talked about? I was confused because I did feel warmth toward Alec, he was funny and sweet, and we were undeniably compatible. But suddenly, I knew I didn't *want* him. What was I going to do?

Shots of Ouzo awaited me as I came out of the bathroom, and I shoved my questions aside for the rest of the night.

The club wasn't busy when we arrived. It was spacious and airy, with glass and cubic zirconia-studded chandeliers and light fixtures decking the dance hall's ceiling and the hallway walls. The bass line in the music thump thump thumped through the venue. I felt at ease there. Everything was dark but also shiny. It was too loud to think or communicate properly, I was simply there taking it all in. The club filled up, and we began to dance.

Alec held me close and pressed me against his body. I rested my chin on his shoulder. Over his shoulder, I began to see other men watching me. They winked at me and held out their hands teasingly as if offering to take me out of Alec's arms. What?! Three days previously, I had received one man's attention, and suddenly, here I had multiple men vying for my time while I was in someone else's arms. I was astounded.

I was wanted.

That moment was my first taste of the magic I am teaching in this book - the power I have to turn my desirability on and be *wanted*. In Alec's arms, I felt safe, I felt seen and valued for who I was, and I felt that I was desirable. At the time, I assumed this magic came from outside myself. Someone else had noticed that I was lovable, which made others notice that I was lovable. In fact, what I had tapped into was an inner knowing. At that moment, *I* knew I was desirable, and other people could tell I knew. I had tapped into the energy of being wanted.

That experience also taught me that I didn't just want to be wanted, I deeply desired to find someone I wanted back wholly and completely. I did not turn my relationship luck around that night in London. I left the country the next day, Alec and I became friends, and I continued to fumble through relationships for another good decade. I made almost every relationship error in the book and learned deep lessons about what I *didn't* want to experience in love. I spent a lot of time wanting love I couldn't have and rejecting the attention I was offered. Much of my energy went into figuring out how to fit myself into love. Most of the time, I concluded that I was either too much or not enough of something to be lovable.

Too Much Not Enough

There are many reasons it is difficult to find love, and most of them have to do with a self-concept that you are either too much or not enough of something to experience love. You may believe you are too fat, too ugly, too sick, too dumb, too demanding, too needy, or too picky. When you sense there is something inherently wrong, unlovable, or undesirable about you, you will behave in strange ways during dating. You might experience brain fog, the feeling that you don't know what to think, say or do. You may avoid the search for love entirely. Perhaps you spend lots of energy on romantic drama because you are constantly using dating as a playground to live out your fears about whether you are worth loving.

Another belief that makes dating difficult is that something outside of you stops you from having love. You tell yourself that there are no good men left or that no good man out there wants you. You'll think it's too difficult to meet someone, given where you live geographically. You believe the odds are stacked against you. Either way, your negative view of yourself or the dating world pervades your dating experience.

Negative beliefs are insidious. You will never run out of reasons that you or your life are too much or not enough of something. After meeting Alec, I began to accept the idea that I might be physically attractive enough to get asked out on dates. But then, the original fear that I was unattractive turned into the belief that I was attractive enough for sex but not for a relationship beyond sex. With more experience came the worries that I wasn't good enough, smart enough, fun enough, interesting enough, and successful enough to be in a loving, committed relationship. Your own brain will come up with all kinds of reasons why the love you want isn't happening for you. In your logical, survival-focused mind, you can always be both too much and not enough for love.

All of your beliefs affect your energy around dating. When your brain says that dating means getting low-quality matches, having countless boring first conversations, being used for sex, and being discarded, it's natural for dating to feel like an exhausting and hopeless endeavor. You don't show up as your best self when you think and feel this way about looking for love. While your brain is busy draining your dating energy, it hides one major truth from you. The truth is that great dating is about connection, and you already have the power to connect.

The Power to Connect

The drive to survive is buried in our DNA and hormonal systems. That drive includes our desire to connect and procreate. The drive shows up in life as the desire to be loved or be in connection. You are alive because of the connection and nurturing you received as an infant. Some people got the short end of the stick when it came to the nurturing received as an infant. You may have learned ways to survive and receive attention, love, and care as a small child that may or may not have been healthy. No matter what your early childhood looked like, you have spent your entire life thus far creating different kinds of connections with people in order to survive and thrive as a human. In other words, the fact that you are alive proves you have the power to connect. You wouldn't be here without it.

Now, you have habits and strategies you have learned and use to connect with others, and some of those habits are probably very effective. However, some of them may be ineffective for creating romantic connections. Many of us tend to get anxious, competitive, or downright weird when it comes to relationships with sexual potential. No matter what you have learned about connection, you can unlearn what doesn't work and relearn or deepen successful strategies. Humans are learning creatures. Your previous experience of love, connection, and care does not disqualify you from having a big, heart-filling, love-quenching romance. You learned connection once, and you can learn it again. It is a skill that can be studied, improved, and mastered.

Working with feminine energy will transform your feelings, sensations, assumptions, and habits around connection. You will become aware of your own energy, which will change your connection to yourself. Once you are connected to yourself, allowing emotional connection with your dates will begin to feel much more possible, bearable, and enjoyable. Embodying the seven feminine energy shifts of seduction will unlock your power around romantic and sexual connection. My guess is you are more attractive and lovable than you can currently imagine. What you need to do is shift your energy and practice the skills of seduction. The first step in strengthening your ability to connect in dating and be wanted is to get acquainted with what *you* really want - your deepest desire.

Exercise: Discovering Your Deepest Desire

Attraction begins with desire; the most important desire when creating a relationship is your own. We'll start there. Let's look at your personal desire for a romantic relationship.

Before I discovered the art of feminine seduction, I didn't know what I was looking for with men. I was striking in the dark and coming out disappointed every time. I thought I was just looking for someone great who wanted me. I wasn't very specific about when, where, why, and how long we would be together. I consistently attracted relationships that went nowhere and left me feeling empty. It doesn't have to be like that. You get to claim what you *want* to experience.

Get deeply in touch with what you're looking for in a relationship so that you know it when you see it and so you know when you haven't found it. We are looking for diamond clarity in your vision. If you close your eyes and imagine your future lover or lovers, you can feel their presence near you.

What do you want to experience in love? Write it down. You can also draw, paint, sculpt, collage, haiku, bake a representative cake, or compose it into a song. I only request that you create something in the 3rd dimension about it. Get your vision somewhere visible, audible, or tangible. Construct your Vision of Love. Create your ask for relationship. Get specific. Your vision points out your values, standards, priorities, and goals. Clarity helps you get what you want in any goal, and romance is no different.

This exercise is the perfect starting point for a successful seduction because it primes your brain to look for the kind of person you desire. If your mind doesn't know what to look for, it won't necessarily zero in on your person, even if he crosses your path. Imagine you're at the grocery store and your dream partner is behind you in line, but you're too busy deciding whether you need that bar of Toblerone to notice he's there! Get connected to your vision so your mind is primed. Also, when you're truly rock solid about what you're looking for in a relationship and what it looks and feels like, it's much harder to fall into unhealthy relationship patterns and accept less than you truly desire.

Here are example questions to consider for your Vision of Love:

What does your partner look like?

How do they carry themselves?

What do they like?

How do they spend their time?

What do you do together?

What do you talk about?

What values do you share?

What do they do, say, or give that lets you know they love you?

How do you feel in their presence?

What kind(s) of sex do you have?

What kind of relationship do you want with them? (Committed? Open? Legal Marriage?)

What kind of future do you want with them? (Children? Retirement? You build a van and travel the Australian continent?)

Creating your Vision of Love is a move your brain may find threatening. It may respond by coming up with objections to this exercise. Here are things that have come up for women in my program around their visions:

"I'm not attractive, so I can't expect my partner to be super hot."

"I'm not my physical fittest, so I don't want to put down 'has a good body' under looks."

"I don't want to define my ideal too exactly in case I'm wrong when I meet someone."

"I haven't had sex yet, so I don't know what I like."

"What if I don't care what he does in his spare time?"

Almost always, the underlying thought is: *I don't deserve this*, or *This isn't possible*. Don't worry about what your brain or past experience tells you is possible or impossible. What you are doing in this exercise is getting in touch with your own deepest desire and your ability to observe and claim what you want. Your current reality isn't a factor in this exercise. Your only focus is your deepest desire. What matters is what you want.

Here's a little secret to soothe your doubting mind. You are not creating a checklist of qualities and categories to judge your dates by. You are not about to reject men who don't have the hair color of your dreams. Your vision is about you. You are creating a connection to your own sense of desire. Your profound desires, your perhaps unspoken, secret thoughts. You want to uncover cravings you have buried. You never have to show your vision to anyone. You can even burn it if that makes you more comfortable. It is your fantasy. It is your personal dream. It is not constricted by 3-dimensional reality, practicality, your past experience of love and attention, or the things your mother said to you when you were young. This vision is your deepest desire set free. The only goal is to get in touch with what you want and be honest about it.

I recommend doing this exercise at least once a month, perhaps more often at the beginning, if connecting to your desires is difficult for you. Go slowly and gently if this exercise brings up any fear or pain. You will often find your desires morph, shrink, or expand over time. Continue to create diamond clarity around the kind of love you want to experience. When you know what you want, you are so much more likely to create it.

TL;DR (Too Long; Didn't Read)

1. Your personality and appearance are not what determine your attractiveness and seductiveness. Your energy is.

2. No matter who you are, you can become a great seductress - someone who gets what she wants in love.

3. Great seductresses come in all shapes, sizes, and personalities.

4. The way to become a great seductress is to shift your energy.

5. Your brain will come up with all kinds of reasons why you are unlovable or won't be able to find love. Don't believe everything

your brain tells you; you can always learn new energies, habits, and ways of connecting.

6. You already have the power to connect, and you can unlearn what doesn't work and relearn or deepen successful strategies.

7. Desire is the first step in attraction and becoming a great seductress; the most important desire is your own.

8. Get in touch with your desire for a relationship by constructing your vision of love.

CHAPTER 2

HOW TO CREATE LOVE

You have the power to create love. Shifting into your feminine energy is an essential step in being able to experience love with anyone. Next, you'll need to learn the skills of creating love, which I call seduction. The process of seduction gives you the power to create love whenever you want. You need three ingredients for a successful seduction:

1. Attraction
2. Sexual Tension
3. Emotional Connection

You can create all three of these experiences intentionally while dating. You don't need to rely on your perfect match riding in on a white horse and sweeping you off your feet. It's alright if the idea of creating these seduction ingredients with someone sounds like a mystery right now. You're in the right place. You will learn the skills of these ingredients through the energy shifts and dating techniques outlined in this book.

Attraction

We'll begin with attraction. Attraction is the moment you take notice of someone and you feel interested. It is the moment you see someone across the room or on your device, and you feel the intrigue bubble up. There is something about their smile, their presence, their gestures, their words.

Attraction can also be the moment in a conversation when your interest is peaked. It is a moment of heat or quick warmth. Suddenly, you're paying attention. In the movies, we often see attraction played out as the moment a man sees a woman walking down the stairs in her effortlessly stunning ball gown or mini dress. It can be that. But it doesn't have to be. There are as many ways to ignite attraction as there are people on earth. You will become more attractive (magnetic) by applying feminine energy shifts in your life. People will begin to notice you at the grocery store, as you walk down the street, or at events and gatherings. Because of your energy, people will take notice of you and feel intrigued.

Heat

The most immediate heated attraction I ever experienced was Martin. I first saw him on the street of a small village in the wine country of Germany. After I left Alec in London, I moved to the village to work as a nanny for a 4-year-old and a 6-month-old infant. It was late summer in the wine country, and the village was hosting a harvest festival. Colorful booths lined the cobblestone streets selling sausages, french fries, and heart-shaped cookies decorated with romantic or friendship messages in pastel-colored icing. They were keepsake cookies, not for eating.

On a hot Friday, I took the children to the festival. We walked down a street of splashy booths to find a ride called a ship swing. The 4-year-old wanted a turn. I gave the ride attendant our tickets, and we climbed into the rowboat-sized swing. The attendant pushed us back as far as he could, and we were off sailing through the sky. Like a normal swing, I could manipulate the motion and intensity of our boat with my body by holding onto the chains that held us up and arching my spine back and forth with the swing's pull and release.

As we swung, a young man walked confidently up to the ride holding the hand of a little boy. He had dark hair and skin the color of a latte; he seemed to gleam in the sun. He was muscular, and he moved with a purposeful swagger. I was immediately on alert. The attendant put the dark-haired man and the boy in the swing next to us and pushed them off.

The dark-haired man stood up in their little boat and began to swing them higher and higher, using the force of his whole body to manipulate the ropes. I watched him from the corner of my eye as I gently swung our little boat back and forth with the motion of my seated body.

"He's swinging so high!" my charge called out loudly.

"Yes," I agreed, "very high."

I knew he could hear us talking about him and felt immediately self-conscious. When our turn ended and we got off the swing, I took one more glance in the man's direction and then re-focused on getting the kids ice cream. But the impression had been made. Attraction had struck.

You Can Create Attraction

Attraction is intrigue, interest, and curiosity. It ignites like a spark. It's the feeling you experience when you meet someone you want to know more about. You can tell there is something is interesting, attractive, or otherwise compelling about them. You may get the urge to say something to them, or you may go into your head and fantasize about what you *would* say to them if you dared.

Hormonally, this step is all about dopamine and serotonin. Dopamine is the "pleasure" hormone - released when you eat chocolate, listen to your favorite song, go shopping - anything that gets you excited or motivates you. Serotonin is similar, but it also creates a sense of calm and focus in your mind.

Attraction feels good in your body and says *there is something special about this connection*. Here's the potentially mind-blowing part: You can create attraction. The biochemical response of pleasure in the human body and mind rules the spark of interest. You can become someone who sticks around as pleasant in someone else's mind. You can become difficult to forget.

Spark

But there I was, oblivious of any dopamine or serotonin coursing through my veins on the Friday of the festival. I walked the children home feeding them ice cream and wiping their faces. Several times that afternoon, my mind replayed the dark-haired man striding confidently toward the ship swings. Who was he? He was, of course, Martin.

Night fell, and the adult portion of the town festival began. An outdoor disco dance party graced a grassy field, complete with a fake wooden dance floor under a huge tent, a beer counter, picnic tables, and porta potties. I arrived at the party with an American friend and scouted the venue. We went to the beer counter and ordered poorly because, as American teens, we had minimal experience ordering alcoholic beverages. I actually preferred plain water over flavored drinks. The bartender recommended that I get the local specialty— red wine with coca cola. I accepted, despite not liking either. It was surprisingly delicious, the sweetness of the coke balancing the sourness I disliked about the wine and the wine toning down the bubbles I disliked about the soda.

The party was full tilt, with dance tunes and loud chatter filling the tent and echoing over the fields and hills of grape vines. My friend and I watched the dance floor for a while, sipping our drinks, and then I saw him, the man from the ship swing. He was standing alone on the other side of the dance floor, casually and coolly drinking a beer. Was he married? Was he a father? Had he noticed me earlier? My brain went into overdrive with questions, drowning out my awareness of the music and the crowd. I continued working on my drink and chatting with my friend while watching him from the corner of my eye.

By the time my drink was just about gone, no one had come to join him. He steadily watched the dancing. Then, just once, when I glanced across the dance floor, he glanced back at me, and we both smiled. His smile seemed somewhat naughty. My heartbeat quickened. A shiver went up my spine, and heat spread through my entire body. The attraction was intense. I sensed that something needed to be done about it. With our drinks empty, my friend and I returned our glasses (you were paid to return them yourself). Then she ventured outside to the porta potties set up for the festival. I didn't want to join her. This was my chance. I was quite a lightweight, and the one drink had put me over the edge of intoxication. With the wine and sugar lending me confidence and my heart pounding out of my chest, I idled across the dance floor to where he still stood.

"Do you have children?" I blurted out.

"What?" He said, not having heard me over the music.

He stepped closer to me and leaned his ear down to my mouth.

"Hi," I said, feeling overwhelmed by his presence, "those weren't my children earlier. Was that your son?" Somehow, I couldn't stop myself from being so forward.

"No," he replied, "my cousin."

"Oh, nice," I said.

"I'm Martin," he said.

"Alana," I responded. We didn't shake hands. I was unsure what I was doing, and he didn't offer a hand.

"Do you want a drink?" he asked.

"Yes," I said, nodding.

And I followed him to the beer counter.

We chatted slowly and casually as we waited for our drinks and then got them. He didn't speak any English and only a limited amount of German, so our conversation was stilted. All I could understand was that he was Slovakian and was in Germany to work in his uncle's "garden." That explained the deep tan and the muscles.

"Do you want to dance?" he asked me.

This man. Surely now I was in the plot of a romantic comedy. I surrendered to it fully.

"Yes," I replied, and we set down our drinks.

He took me in his arms, and we danced. I could smell his cologne as I leaned against him, a rich, earthy, luxurious scent that moved all the way to the back of my head. His hands held me firmly, and his body moved confidently and sensually with mine. I was no longer thinking or trying to make sense of love. I no longer cared where I was or what was coming next in life; all I could sense was being there in his arms. I was in the locked embrace of sexual tension.

You Can Create Sexual Tension

In exchanging words and gestures, Martin and I moved to the second step of romantic love: sexual tension. Sexual tension creates sexual desire or lust in the connection. The sexual hormones of testosterone and estrogen govern the chemistry of a connection. Feminine energy practices support estrogen-predominant people to feel more sexual arousal and desire in themselves. Practicing feminine energy dating also encourages your masculine partner to *act* more and *give* more, activities that help boost testosterone. In other words, allowing testosterone-predominant people to act from that masculine energy gives them better access to their desire or lust, while embodying feminine energy helps you get in touch with yours. When you both feel that chemistry inside you, you'll find sexual tension easily escalates.

You want some sexual tension to be present in any romantic or sexual connection because that energy differentiates a friend or acquaintance from a lover. You do not need to have sex or withhold sex to create sexual tension. Likewise, you do not need to play games around physical contact or sex to create sexual tension.

Creating sexual tension is about the *suggestion* or *emotion* of sex. You can generate it in several different ways and on several levels through speaking, physical contact, or gestures. For example, when Martin glanced at me and smiled naughtily across the dance floor, a small amount of sexual tension grew between us. When we danced pressed against each other, we created a large amount of sexual tension. On the intense end of the spectrum, engaging in sexual foreplay without orgasm produces a lot of sexual tension.

Flirtation is the most straightforward way to create sexual tension in dating. It is a skill discussed in Chapter 7. In simplest terms, flirtation is letting someone know you like them. Like sexual tension, flirtation exists on a spectrum. Sometimes you are politely telling someone what makes them great, and other times you are telling someone that you find them sexually irresistible. Clients often come to me with blocks around flirtation because even the act of letting someone know they are interesting can feel too vulnerable and scary. The good news is that there are many ways to work through a fear of or hesitancy around flirtation. Remember that at its heart, flirtation is just telling someone you think they're great, and most people love to hear that about themselves.

When it comes to sexual tension, you have the power to create as much or as little, as fast or as slow, and as subtly or as obviously as you like. Most often, during the seduction process, you will create sexual tension through flirtation. You can come on strong if that's your style, or you can be very mysterious, flirting a little or a lot. You will learn more about the skill of creating sexual tension throughout this book, but for now, it's important to understand that you need it to create a romantic connection with a potential partner.

Attachment

Dancing so close to Martin's body created sexual tension in me. I wanted him closer and closer to my body. I wanted to know more about him. I eventually snapped out of the bubble of our dancing and noticed that my friend was back and waiting at the edge of the dance floor. I pulled Martin over to her.

"This is Martin," I said, "We saw each other at the festival earlier and just met."

"Looks like you know each other pretty well now," she said, smirking because she had seen how we were dancing right after meeting.

I was too intoxicated and happy to feel the shame that usually crept in when anyone noticed me as a romantic or sexual being. We went to a table outside and sat down with our drinks. My friend met some new people, and they were all cheerfully talking while Martin and I murmured together in our broken German. As the night progressed, I got cold, and he gave me the shirt off his back. He sat there with his white undershirt shining in the dark while the faint party lights glowed on his exposed muscles.

Then, he kissed me. This was a new kind of kiss for me. His mouth was warm, confidently slow, and disarmingly sweet. Here were the fireworks and heart palpitations everyone talked about. I was breathless. And I was not cold anymore. Then, he pulled back and said he needed to use the bathroom. He got up and crossed the grass. Several dance songs went by, and he did not return. I circled the party looking for him, at least to give his shirt back, I reasoned. But he was nowhere to be seen. Suddenly, I felt rejected and did not feel like partying anymore, so we left soon after. Back home, with my friend asleep, I buried my face in his shirt, inhaling his distinctive scent and cologne.

I daydreamed about him all the next day, imagining what would happen when I gave him his shirt back and beyond. Would he be at the festival again that night? What would he say about his disappearance? I imagined all kinds of romantic scenarios and how much he would love me. I became attached to the idea of our love affair.

The next night, I made my way down cobblestone streets back to the festival field, holding Martin's shirt. He was there surrounded by his family and I was completely alone. I realized I would have to go up to him in front of all of them. As someone with lots of can-do energy, I walked up to the unknown group and tried to be subtle about returning the shirt to Martin. His family, unfortunately, was very interested in our exchange. They all stopped their conversations to laugh and clap him on the back. Then they told him to buy me a drink. He did not seem that interested in talking to me, but he went off to get me a drink.

An older cousin of his took an interest in me and struck up a conversation about who I was and what I was doing in this tiny German town. I was so distracted thinking about Martin and his behavior I couldn't focus on her questions, even though she was a potential friend and I needed friends. Finally, late in the evening, I got a moment alone with him.

"Where did you go last night?" I asked.

"Home," he said, "I got cold. I went to get a coat, but I guess I fell asleep."

That made sense. I could have done the same thing. He barely made eye contact with me and didn't initiate further conversation, which made me feel incredibly unimportant and confused. Just yesterday, we had been dancing passionately and making out. Now he didn't seem interested in me at all. I wasn't sure where I had gone wrong, but I told myself he wasn't interested, and we parted ways without exchanging numbers. Once again, I was leaving the party feeling rejected and let down by love.

"We should hang out!" his cousin exclaimed when I indicated I was leaving.

I agreed. Though my heart felt like it had a dozen tiny needles in it from Martin's apathy toward me, I consoled myself with the idea of having a friend. I wrote my number on her arm with a sharpie. Weeks passed, and I received a text, but it wasn't from the cousin.

"Hello, Elena. It is Martin. My birthday is on Tuesday and I want to invite you."

My heart leaped out of my chest, and I jumped off the couch. I paced nervously around the room. Here he is! Maybe I was wrong. Maybe he does like me. He doesn't really know my name but must have gotten my number from his cousin. That took some effort. Somehow, he knew his cousin had my number and asked her for it. I saw it as a sign that he cared. Suddenly life was exciting again. Only,

I was supposed to go away for three days, including Tuesday. The thought of canceling the trip with my friend crossed my mind. But no, that was excessive and unfair to her. My heart ached, but I knew what I had to do.

I am sorry, I will be in Frankfurt on Tuesday. I hope you have a great party. I wrote. The words felt heavy.

"Thank you." He wrote back.

Nothing else came. Was he angry or disappointed in me? I tried to guess his emotional response. I thought about him my entire trip to Frankfurt. I struggled to be present and have fun. I wanted to be somewhere else.

"Happy birthday," I wrote to him on the day.

"Thank you," he wrote again, but he asked me out this time.

Now we were getting somewhere. We met at his apartment. It was built in the loft of an old farm complex. The living room had a soft gray couch and a TV with a practical kitchenette off to the side, and then there was a cozy bedroom with a slanted ceiling just under the roof and a small bathroom. We played video games on his couch, and he made fun of my uselessness with the controller. Then he kissed me like nobody's business. I let him undress me, and then he went down on me. I protested, he insisted, and I surrendered. It was the beginning of my education in pleasure.

He was very giving and so kind to me in bed. Then when we were apart, it was like he disappeared completely. No texts, no calls. From this behavior, I assumed that all he wanted from me was sex. I felt very apprehensive about penetrational sex and was sure I wasn't ready for it. But I couldn't stop seeing him, kissing him, letting him pleasure me, and wanting him more.

I invited him out when some American friends visited, and then I went home with him instead of them. He became an addiction that I couldn't stop thinking about or indulging.

After a second night out with my friends, we walked home from the late bus, and I watched as he flirted physically with my friend, who graciously flirted back. I watched quietly from 20 feet back as they skipped and chased each other, eventually rolling around wrestling on the ground. *Well, who could blame him? She had blonder hair, bigger boobs, and a brighter personality than me. I would never be that attractive.* My pride and feelings were, perhaps, irrevocably hurt, and I went home with my friends instead of Martin. But minutes after we walked in the door, he texted that he wanted me, and I went to him, hurt pride and all. Only that night, I began to feel smaller. I began to realize that because I wasn't so beautiful, he might never fully want me, even if I did sleep with him.

He went back to his hometown for a week and didn't contact me when he returned. Then, I noticed him commenting on the Facebook pictures of a girl from his hometown. I translated every comment. He seemed to be insulting her, telling her the bags under her eyes made her look like an elephant. I knew I was pathetic for stalking her on Facebook and for wanting a man who used insults to flirt.

After two weeks, I reached out to him again, but he gave a non-committal answer. He wasn't interested in seeing me. I couldn't judge him. The way I saw it, he had made it clear that he wanted sex, and I had made it clear that I didn't. I did not think about the way I was showing up with my hurt pride and indifference while never once telling him what I felt or wanted.

Christmas came and went. The world was frozen white. Christmas markets full of white lights and the smell of hot mulled wine warmed every city. Holiday magic hung in the air, but without Martin in my life, the season carried the magic of death. I saw bare, frozen earth everywhere. I was like an addict in withdrawal. Nothing was as good as being with him. But I told myself I couldn't have him and that I had to let him go.

I was asked out on a date by a man I met while using Germany's organized hitchhiking service, *Mitfahrgelegenheit*. He took me out to lunch. When we got to his flashy car, he opened the trunk, took out a pair of tennis shoes, and changed into them to drive. When we parked near the restaurant, he put his leather street shoes back on. It seemed like a show rather than a genuine need for different footwear, and I found it incredibly vain and repulsive. I immediately wished I was off with Martin, who was decidedly unpretentious.

As we got in the car for him to drive me home, the shoe changer asked, "Will you do me a favor?"

"That depends," I responded coolly.

He laughed and laughed, and I was silent. He kept laughing as we turned onto the freeway and sped up.

"So, what is it?" I asked when he had calmed himself.

"Will you kiss me?" he asked.

"No," I said, and then he argued with me all the way down the highway, making me wonder how dangerous it would be to jump out of the car at that speed.

I missed Martin deeply. I couldn't imagine being with someone else. I had never known someone so intimately with my body. And I spent 80 hours a week with small children, one of whom didn't speak, so I was incredibly lonely and intellectually bored. So finally, a month later, I swallowed my pride and texted Martin.

"Hi, how are you?" I started.

He wrote back quite quickly.

"I'm good, you?"

"I'm good. Can I see you?"

We arranged to meet the next night. He met me with all the passion of a lover who had been kept away for months. And his mouth still tasted as sweet as I remembered. We attempted to sleep together. Only we couldn't because I was too tight.

"This has to come out," he said, poking up my vaginal wall with a finger.

I didn't know enough about female anatomy to know what was happening. All I knew was incredible pain when he tried to penetrate me, even with a finger. I had no idea what was wrong or what to do.

We lay close to each other. He did not make me feel ashamed that we weren't having sex. He didn't pressure me at all, something that I later learned was an incredible gift for a man to give a woman. The loneliness in both of us was palpable as we muddled through conversation. We were both young, overworked, and stranded far from our own languages and cultures. He asked me to translate the words of an English song into German for him. He told me he had come to this town to work for his family because he had been unable to get a good job in his country. He had failed out of school after refusing to sleep with a teacher. I wasn't entirely sure what to make of his life story, and I likely misunderstood parts of it. We communicated what we could in words and left the rest to physical touch. In the morning, I woke up in his arms. I felt ashamed that I seemed incapable of sex but overjoyed to be near his skin.

I went to a local gynecologist who told me she could remove my hymen. She also gave me birth control. I took the birth control pills but refused the surgery. It seemed drastic. The next week, I discussed her diagnosis as best I could with Martin, sitting cross-legged on his gray couch while hugging a pillow. We had penetrational sex that night. He moved patiently and slowly, and my pain subsided after a short time in his arms.

After sex, we lay naked next to each other and talked. Laughing softly, he told me the story of how he had gone out in a tractor but gotten too drunk to drive it home, and someone had had to come to get him. Then Martin forgot where the tractor was when he was supposed to go get it the next day. I slowly began to see a common thread in his stories of drinking and forgetting. Forgetting--a clear sign of alcoholism.

We began to see each other about once a week in the dark of night. He would drive me home at dawn just before our households awoke. It was a nice ritual, our meeting and sleeping together, and it was the only thing keeping me happy in my life of childcare. I thought about him obsessively as I did the menial tasks of my daily life. Feeding.

Ironing. More feeding. School pick-ups. Repeat. Once a week, my life was special in Martin's bed.

Then the warm weather came, and he disappeared without a word. He stopped responding to texts and calls. I wasn't brave enough to go down to his family's complex in the village and knock on his door. Then, a photo of the woman with the elephant eyes smiling from his uncle's tractor popped up on Facebook. I knew I had to let him go this time, no matter how much it hurt. He could drink and forget me, but I couldn't forget him.

You Can Create Emotional Connection

Step number three of any great seduction is creating an emotional bond. This is what I failed to do with Martin. I created a deep attachment to him on my side, making it feel like I needed him. Even though I didn't actually know him well, I felt very attached to him. I had gone on my own emotional journey while dating him, experiencing the pure joy of our very first encounter, then what I perceived as rejection, then elation when he reached out again, the pleasure of his kisses and touch, confusion when he disappeared, all the emotional turmoil of becoming sexual with him, and finally heartbreak at his grand disappearance.

To this day, I do not know his emotional experience of meeting and being with me. I can say that he did not attach to me the way I attached to him. Why didn't he? Potentially, alcohol got in the way, but definitely, he didn't attach to me because we didn't share a deep emotional connection. Attachment can be one-sided. Connection requires two people to feel into the experience of the other. If we had had a healthy emotional connection, I would know what he felt for me, and I would have had some idea of what the experience of knowing me was like for him.

Emotional connection requires sharing emotions instead of developing them alone through fantasy and assumptions. Connection is not riding your own emotional rollercoaster through a relationship while never sharing your thoughts or feelings with the other person involved. Instead, connection is what actually happens between the two of you. Emotional connection is the experience the two of you create together. Blame it on our language barriers or the blockade of ice I had constructed around my heart. Martin and I did not have the mutual connection of trust and familiarity that is necessary for an attraction that lasts.

Creating an emotional connection is about trust and the feeling of really *knowing* someone. It is about sharing who you are and what you genuinely think and feel with another person. When you connect with someone at this level, you create an emotional bond with them. Martin and I fell short of this.

Many processes govern emotional bonding in the body, and the primary hormones we know relate to human bonding are oxytocin and vasopressin. For example, when you gently stroke your arm, you may feel the effect of oxytocin releasing. It is a calming, loving sensory response, which also happens as the result of hugging, snuggling, or having hot sex. Vasopressin helps regulate many blood-related processes, so it is involved in many areas of your life, including heart rate, memory, and emotion.

A budding relationship needs emotional connection to create a meaningful bond rather than a one-sided attachment. When I was dating Martin, I believed emotional connection was a matter of luck, time, or compatibility, rather than emotion. While luck, time, and compatibility will help you out with emotional connection, you also have sovereignty over your emotional presence on dates. That's why I recommend creating opportunities for emotional connection rather than hoping to get lucky or find someone compatible. Claim your agency around connecting emotionally. You can connect with any willing partner, and that emotional connection tends to make you lucky, compatible, and right on time for love.

Although a great deal of sexual shame blocked me from creating attraction and sexual tension in early dating, fear of emotional connection took me the longest to overcome. That said, overcoming my resistance to all the ingredients of a romantic relationship was relatively easy when I got down to it. Focusing on your feminine energy allows you to bring your natural self and magnetism forward in romance while soothing the parts of yourself that are afraid of intimacy. Engaging in emotionally intimate conversation can be more straightforward and painless than you currently imagine. For me, the most significant shift around connecting with dates was this: intimacy doesn't have to mean bearing your eternal soul to a near stranger. You can start very modestly with what you share about yourself. I will teach you my emotional communication technique in Chapter 8. It is a no-fail, all-levels-friendly way to create an emotional connection from the very first moment you meet a potential love interest. All seven energetic shifts in this book will help you relax, feel safer in yourself, open up, treat your dates as emotionally trustworthy, and therefore communicate more vulnerably and honestly. Emotional connection mastery is just a few energetic shifts away!

Exercise: Diagnose Your Love Block

Here is a quick test to diagnose which of the three ingredients is your biggest block in creating your dream relationship.

1. If you rarely or never receive romantic attention (you don't receive suggestive smiles, don't get flirted with, don't get asked out, etc.), the most important place for you to focus first is on *Attraction.* The first three feminine energy shifts (Chapters 4, 5, and 6) are the most important in terms of attraction. Therefore, I recommend mastering those fundamentals.

2. If you rarely or never make it past first contact or first date(s), your biggest struggle is *Sexual Tension.* Feminine energy shifts three and four (Chapters 6 and 7) will support you in moving through your discomfort and confusion around sexual tension. Spend extra time and attention on the skills taught in those chapters.

3. Suppose you rarely or never make it past a certain time or commitment marker (One month, three months, exclusivity, commitment, etc.). In that case, *Emotional Connection* is what will take your love life to the next level. All the feminine energy shifts will help you here, but shifts four, five, six, and seven (Chapters 7, 8, 9, and 10) are significant. Give them a little extra love as you add feminine energy to your dating life.

Each of the three steps - attraction, sexual tension, and emotional connection - is an important ingredient for feminine seduction. You will want to master each of them to whatever degree is right for you. When I say right for you, I mean right for your natural way of being in the world today. For example, if you have a lot of sexual energy, you will likely have no problem creating sexual tension with others. On the other hand, if you feel like a beginner at sexual energy, or even a little afraid of it, that's okay, too. Your best match may be someone with less libido *or* who awakens you sexually in a way you've never considered. There are people with all kinds of sexual and emotional needs out there. When you've stepped into your full seductress power, you will attract the best matches for your true being, and you'll feel simply divine.

Be aware, however, that if you feel stuck in dating or dissatisfied with what has happened in your love life so far, you will almost certainly need to confront things that scare you or make you uncomfortable. If the idea of flirting with someone makes your stomach turn, dates or interactions with you will be missing crucial sexual tension. If opening up with someone new makes you squirm, a lack of emotional connection is probably what's missing from your current approach to romance. Don't worry; we will work through all the common areas of shame and fear around building intimate relationships. Feminine energy is a powerful tool for healing and re-wiring your fears; all the energy shifts will help you face new situations in life. You won't have to change your personality, but you might have to change your habits.

TL;DR

1. There are three steps or ingredients in a successful seduction: 1: attraction, 2: sexual tension, and 3: emotional connection.

2. Each of these ingredients is related to important physiological responses that are part of the human journey of falling in love.

3. You have the power to create all of these ingredients in yourself and to encourage them to bubble up in other people.

4. The seven feminine energy shifts of being, receiving, physicality, wildness, emotion, pace, and process will support you in creating all of these steps.

5. If you rarely or never receive romantic attention, your first priority is ingredient 1: attraction.

6. If you rarely or never make it past the first few dates, your best focus is on ingredient 2: Sexual Tension.

7. If you rarely or never make it past a specific dating marker (i.e., the first time you sleep together, three months of casual dating, exclusivity, one year, etc.), your most important focus is ingredient 3: emotional connection.

8. Becoming a great seductress can be more straightforward and painless than you currently imagine.

CHAPTER 3

TRUST YOURSELF FIRST

Faery Tale Love Story

Once upon a time, in most faery tales across cultures, there existed a dynamic between male characters and female characters. In each of these tales, the male hero's task is to overcome obstacles, save the female heroine, and win her hand in marriage. Modern rewrites of these stories attempt to correct females being portrayed as "helpless victims, mere trophies, in need of saving." However, I propose to you that these stories are not intended to be read literally. They are not intended to point out innate capacities involved in being a "man" or a "woman."

I propose that rather than teaching us how to live into gender roles, faery tales point to the sacred relationship between masculine and feminine energy in each of us. Feminine energy makes up our inner world, while masculine energy is the power we extend externally, mostly meaning our words and actions. In this interpretation, all people have both energies. All people have the energy of their inner world, and all people have the energy they express in the outer world. Masculine energy is not just for male men, nor is feminine energy the sole domain of female women. Energy is energy, not sex, gender, or a fixed part of your personality.

If we interpret the roles of males and females in faery tales as masculine and feminine energy archetypes, they show us a specific relationship: *the highest purpose of masculine energy is to serve feminine energy.* Outward masculine action is intended to rescue, protect, and take care of inner feminine well-being. Personally, I think this interpretation is much more interesting and useful in life than stories of women locked in towers. Energetically speaking, actions ought to serve well-being.

Start your feminine energy dating journey with this understanding: your own masculine energy is intended to serve *your* feminine energy. Your words and actions are intended to serve you. Before you date confidently or with any semblance of sexual power, you must build trust in your masculine energy to act in your best interest. Your masculine energy is responsible for taking care of you externally and speaking your inner truth out loud. Build trust and confidence in yourself by consciously expressing your masculine energy.

Masculine Energy Check

Consider your current relationship to your own masculine energy by answering the following questions for yourself. Do your daily actions support your inner Self to be and feel your best? Do you take exquisite care of yourself?

Here are some specific physical needs to get you thinking about how you relate to taking care of yourself.

1. When you get the inner desire to go outside and breathe some fresh air, do you do it?
2. Do you eat and drink out of hunger, thirst, and pleasure, or does sustaining yourself come from obligation, "should," stress, or maybe "I guess this is what's in the fridge"?
3. Do you rest or re-energize when tired?
4. Does the work you do light you up and utilize your gifts or does it drain the life juice right out of you?

If you still feel unsure whether your masculine energy takes care of your feminine energy, here are some common ways underperforming masculine energy shows up:

1. You don't express your wants and needs.
2. You don't use your voice to assert yourself and your opinions.
3. You say yes to caretaking others before caretaking yourself.
4. You allow others to take credit for your work.
5. You date people who need "saving."
6. You feel the need to prove yourself to dates.
7. You know what your body needs to feel its best (in terms of sustenance, socializing, activity, and rest) but you ignore it or "push through."
8. You're so disconnected from yourself that you don't know what you want or need.

These all indicate that your masculine energy does not serve your inner feminine. Most of these scenarios tell the story of your masculine energy ignoring, disavowing, or even abusing your inner self. Have any of these situations been part of your life story? If yes, you have the opportunity to make a potentially life-changing decision right now. You can use your masculine energy to serve your inner Self starting today.

Why Start with Masculine Energy?

Why are we starting a feminine energy dating journey with so much talk about masculine energy? Two very big reasons.

One - Understanding masculine energy helps clarify feminine energy. Knowing both sides of the energy spectrum will help you remember the shifts better when you apply them in dating. And, armed with the knowledge of both sides, you can create energetic polarity in your dating life. Polarity describes the relationship between two opposite characteristics or tendencies, or in this case, masculine and feminine energies. Polarity creates attraction like the negative and positive poles of a magnet. You probably know about polarity through the proverb "opposites attract," and indeed, that is precisely your aim in seduction. You want to use your sexual energy to attract someone with the polar opposite sexual energy. When masculine energy is present, it attracts feminine energy and vice versa. With the knowledge of what masculine and feminine energies are, you will begin to see them everywhere. For example, my clients find that watching romantic comedies becomes a fun study of masculine and feminine energies at play.

If you struggle in dating, you probably have an imbalance in your personal masculine/feminine energy dynamic. Understanding your own masculine energy will help clean up your habits around relating to others before you even head out to the dating field.

Two - You must understand and use your masculine energy in order to experience healthy romantic relationships. It's essential that you can identify your inner feminine inner needs and wants. It's equally important to be able to express them to your partner with your outward-directed masculine energy. Having sovereignty in your masculine energy is necessary for sustaining a healthy relationship with anyone.

You will become more confident in dating when you have established a relationship with your masculine energy. Having conscious awareness of when you are using your masculine energy and when you are holding back your inner feminine truth will help you make better romantic, sexual, and relationship choices. Being connected to your masculine energy will help you stick up for yourself.

In order to trust a man and allow him to take care of you, you must first trust yourself and take excellent care of yourself. Creating self-trust requires that you do and say what supports your truth during seduction. You may need to tell someone it's over, even though it feels uncomfortable or scary. You may need to leave a bad date even though it seems rude. You will struggle to be truly seductive if you are constantly afraid of what people think and what they will do. That kind of fear means you are fixating on others instead of focusing inward and pulling sexy energy toward yourself. Feeling unsafe does not create sensual energy and will often lead you to make choices you later regret. Practice using your masculine energy to serve your feminine energy. Start with understanding and becoming aware of your masculine power. Learn to take action in service of yourself, and you will find that other people want to take care of you, too. Learn to trust yourself to treat you well, and you will find that trusting a man to love you and treat you well comes naturally.

How To Create Safety For Yourself

Let's talk about safety for a moment. It's important to feel safe while dating, particularly as a feminine person. In heterosexual dating, there is a safety disparity between how men and women perceive the world. Women almost always view the world of men through the lens of potential physical threats. We know that men are generally bigger, we know men tend more toward physical aggression, and we know that men are largely responsible for the harm and death of females close to them. I say this to acknowledge and honor that it is not irrational when you, as a feminine being, don't feel safe dating.

There are many, many reasons women don't feel safe dating. Some of them are logical, as in *he doesn't listen or respond to what I say or request*. Some of them are emotional, as in *I don't feel loved by him*, and some of them are buried unconsciously in your nervous system response (commonly known as your fight, flight, freeze, or fawn response). A nervous system response might be when your throat closes up, and you don't say what you're thinking, or when you say something loud and brash that instigates a fight. It can be as subtle as feeling unattracted to someone because they don't return you to the sensation state you associate with desire, such as anxiety, rejection, or overwhelm. The nervous system can lead you to do, say, or feel things you would never have felt, said, or done if you hadn't been activated. It runs your deep-rooted, usually automatic responses to life. It can be so sneaky you don't even notice you reacted automatically.

It's common to feel emotionally or physically unsafe in dating. We tend to put a lot of pressure on the act of dating, which causes heightened emotional responses to situations. When someone doesn't text you back the hour you thought they should, you may decide they aren't interested, and either text them a string of "check-in" texts or block and delete them from your phone. It is extra easy to go to an extreme place where you can no longer think or act clearly. Everything seems like the beginning or the end of love. My usual MO was taking men's behavior as a sign they weren't interested in me and then testing them to see if I was right. The test was that I would refuse to text them first, waiting to see if they would text or ask me out. Then I would generally make it difficult for them to get to know me. After a week or a month or two, when they inevitably didn't get to know me or ended up with someone else, I told myself, *see, I knew they weren't that interested.* And our connection would end.

You may have spent a lot of time dating with your mind on hyper-alert, looking for every sign, dissecting every word your date said or didn't say and every move he made. You may be aware that you tend to attract and not reject aggressive or emotionally unavailable men. Consciously or not, you likely spend a lot of energy worrying about physical and emotional safety in dating.

One of the reasons that understanding and working with your feminine energy is so powerful in dating is that it helps you recognize and acknowledge when you feel safe or not. With awareness of your feminine being and how you feel, you can act with your masculine energy to protect yourself. Your own masculine energy will need to step up to protect your inner feminine. When you feel discomfort about a person or a date, give that discomfort a voice. Don't go on dates you don't want to go on. Don't stay in chat conversations you don't want to be in. Don't remain in romantic relationships where your needs aren't acknowledged or met. Recognizing and serving your own needs will lead you to deeper trust in yourself. Let your masculine energy serve your inner feminine being. You must become your own champion to trust that someone else will not hurt you.

You will feel safe in dating once you trust yourself to make decisions that keep you safe. If you can't be trusted to take care of your own heart, body, and life, why would you trust someone else to do it? Begin by creating the sacred relationship of masculine service to feminine being within your own life. It may take time to develop the ability to speak your mind honestly and kindly and act in your best interest, even when it conflicts with someone else's emotions. Masculine energy requires skill, meaning you learn it rather than innately being it. Develop your masculine energy by practicing speaking up for yourself and others. Practice taking small actions to serve your own well-being. You can begin your practice with the exercise at the end of this chapter.

A Cautionary Tale

I met Max at an Easter Fire - a German tradition in which people gather around enormous flaming bonfires as night falls before Easter Sunday. I was in the depths of loneliness, having been abandoned by Martin (whom I desperately hoped would show up to the fire) two weeks earlier. Max was the attractive one of a group of male friends who spotted me alone, gazing forlornly into the giant flames. They invited me to their after-party. We played drinking games with vodka and Red Bull, and I, much smaller in stature and weight, got drunk much faster than everyone else there. I had to leave early. I ran into Max on the late bus out of our small village a week later.

"Where are you headed?" he asked.

"Out," I said, "There are no clubs here!" I gestured to our tiny, curving, cobble-stoned streets.

"You haven't been to our club?" He gasped sarcastically.

"What? No," I responded, grinning, "Where is it?"

He described the door on a building at the corner of a crossroads I knew well. I had never recognized it as a bar or pub.

"No way," I said, "I thought I'd been to every bar in town,"

"You're missing the best one," he said. "I can take you there if you want."

"Sure," I said and gave him my number.

We had an easy chemistry, perhaps on my side because I was still lovesick and numb from Martin breaking my heart. With Max, I didn't have to feel very much. We went to the village "club," a small pub with a pool table and an ancient pinball machine.

"They used to have karaoke," Max commented.

Our first date was laid back and smooth. He made me laugh in a way I hadn't laughed with a man before - easy and carefree. I felt that nothing was at stake. I said yes to another date, which was a movie date at his house with sex afterward. Again, penetration was painful and made me bleed, but the pain did subside eventually.

My job ended in a matter of weeks, and I left the country. Max didn't ask me to stay. Back in America, a gynecologist diagnosed me with vaginismus - an affliction that means involuntary muscle spasms make sexual penetration painful. The number of women it affects is unknown because, historically, so few of us have been willing to discuss our sexual nature openly. Nevertheless, the diagnosis explained the pain I experienced with Martin and Max. I was given a set of dilators, which were essentially different-sized dildos stacked inside each other like Russian dolls. I was supposed to spend time with them inserted into my vagina to give my body time to adjust to the sensation of penetration. Unfortunately, I did not enjoy this therapy and mainly ignored the accessories, opting instead for talk therapy, pelvic floor therapy, and only sleeping with men I trusted deeply.

Max and I kept up through inconsistent emails, and when I was returning to Germany the following spring, I let him know. That's when I found myself accepting another date with him.

"It's a surprise," he wrote, *"but wear something sexy."*

I wore a little black dress, tights, and knee-high black boots. I met him outside his house in the village, and we jumped in the car. He drove us in the opposite direction of the nearby cities. We wound through obscure countryside and tiny towns, on and on for what felt like a long time. I got more and more curious. Where were we heading? What kind of place was worth driving this far? At this point, I still trusted him a great deal, and therefore my thinking was that he wanted to take me somewhere so special he was willing to drive a great distance. Thanks to this conclusion, I did not feel too unsafe, though I no longer knew where I was, which led to some uneasiness. By necessity, I placed my trust in Max.

He wouldn't tell me where we were going, but he was excited. Eventually, we came to a large, windowless, boxy building with the words "Dream Palace" written on the side. It was not in a city but near a small town.

It must be some kind of theater, I thought.

We entered the door and came to a box office window where a woman greeted us in black and red lingerie. This was a surprise. Were we there to watch a burlesque show, maybe? Now I was nervous. I didn't know what was going to happen, so my brain went into overdrive. The woman in the box office explained what would happen next. Her speech was slow and leisurely, but it felt like a rapid-fire German dialect to my bewildered mind. I barely understood her as my brain simultaneously tried to figure out where I was, what was going on, and what to do. On an unconscious level, I was busy working out whether I was in danger and what I would do in case of emergency. On a conscious level, I felt highly confused and insecure. We left the window and made our way to a unisex locker room.

"What did she say?" I asked Max urgently.

He explained that there would be a sex show and we could take part in it. At this news, my shock grew deeper. First of all, I was shocked that such a thing existed. The need or want for it had never occurred to me, and my second shock was that I was there. It didn't seem like the kind of place you took a girl who experienced difficult and painful intercourse. What was Max thinking? It definitely seemed like a place you went with someone who had expressed interest in it and agreed to all the terms. Again, overwhelm hijacked my brain and led to a lack of clarity.

"What?" I responded to him meekly. After that, all I could do was laugh nervously. This was a perfect and reasonable time to say no, thank you, I don't want to participate in a sex show, but I didn't take it.

"Yes," he said as if this was all an everyday activity. "If you ever want to leave, just say you have a headache or something. It's only free if we participate."

"What do we participate in?" I asked, with a nervous giggle in my voice.

"It's Gang Bang night," he said, "just undress a little."

Here was another great chance to say, *no way, Jose, are you out of your mind?*

But instead, I didn't. I did as he said and took off my boots and tights. I left my dress on. He stripped down to his underwear, and we went out into the venue.

Every corner and every surface was made for sex. Soft surfaces, hard surfaces, beds, a hot tub with rose petals, and a colorful adult jungle gym. Outside there was a pool and another hot tub, and lounge chairs. Upstairs there was a room with a sex swing. Instead of the usual seat for your butt, it had two straps that you could sit or lie back on and two leg straps you could use to stabilize your pelvic area. This was where the "gang bang" was going to take place.

"What's a gang bang exactly?" I asked, eyeing the swing, my mind continuing its shock and inability to process correctly.

Confusion is a typical response when your brain senses danger. According to Max, all the women would be strapped into the swing for the men to take turns penetrating. Max's answer led to more confusion about why I was there and what Max was thinking. Sure, I was adventurous, but I wasn't sure how he'd gotten the idea that I would like this. I was the only female there besides the woman from the box office, and I was at least 20 years younger than everyone except Max. I was also the only one still fully covered.

Max and I made out a bit on the bed. Naked, middle-aged men showed up to watch us there, so I suggested we explore the jungle gym, a series of padded mats of various shapes, just like at a children's tumbling class. Our audience followed us. This kind of attention was not sexy for me. I made an excuse about wanting to explore the grounds. Exploration felt safer than thinking about anything sexual at that moment. And yet, again, I did not say I had a headache nor ask to leave.

The show was starting. Finally, my tongue regained some composure. I said I didn't want to watch. Max said he did, so I waited downstairs in the lounge booths at the bar while he went upstairs to the velvet room with the swing.

Bernhard, a gentle 40-something divorced man wearing only gray briefs, waited obligingly in the booth with me. After he shared the story of the end of his marriage with me, I found myself telling him how I came to be at the sex club. I hadn't known I was coming here. I hadn't said I wanted to come here, and I didn't believe I was the type of woman who gave the impression I was into public sex. Bernhard listened intently and non-judgmentally.

His hair was entirely gray but thick and smartly trimmed. His face had only faint wrinkles coming in, and his skin was generally nice and tan, covering a fit body. I found myself thinking I could make out with him to get back at Max for bringing me to a sex club. Maybe that would teach him that he wasn't into sharing me and make him regret his actions. Speaking to Bernhard reminded me that I wasn't alone in the world with Max and allowed me to get just angry enough to remember who I was and what I wanted and didn't want.

Max came down the stairs. "Honey," he called out, "are you feeling any better?"

"I'm not sick, Max," I said. Then, I gestured to Bernhard, "I told him everything. He knows I'm not sick. I'm ready to go."

Here it was, the moment I finally said what I meant. I had to pass through shock, overwhelm, confusion, and then anger to reach clarity in my thoughts and say what I meant. We left without participating and without paying the lingerie-d woman from the box office. She was upstairs in the swing as we let ourselves out.

While I blamed Max for the evening, it was, in fact, I who did not state my boundaries from the first moment. I could have told him I only wanted a date near our hometown which was near the local bus service. When we pulled up to a mysteriously marked warehouse, I could have asked more questions. I could have said *no* the moment I heard his evening plans. I had never expressed interest in non-monogamous or even kinky sex. This was my truth. But Max was doing what he wanted from his own truth, and he was not really considering mine. And when all was said and done, I also didn't insist that my wants and needs were important and say, *No*.

On the way back to our village, I was still nervous and laughed, trying to deflect it. This is what is known as a fawning response. If you do not feel safe, you may find yourself trying to please - fawn over - the person you are with, to prevent them from getting angry and doing something unpleasant to you. Though my relationship with Max had begun with a lot of trust and safety, he turned the tables on me that night. I had been to his house, I had trusted him with my body, I had trusted him to plan a surprise date for me, and I assumed he would choose something I enjoyed. It turned out he had at least misunderstood who I was and at most, was willing to disregard me in the relationship. I no longer felt confident I knew who he was or what he was capable of. Laughing was the only way to cut through the tension and emotion I was experiencing.

"What a place," I laughed, "I can't believe you took me there."

On the ride home, it came out that Max, in fact, already had a girlfriend. *I didn't ask to get out of the car.* It came out that he lived with her in an apartment in the city and had just let me believe he lived at home with his parents. Again, *I didn't yell at him and ask him to get out of the car.* I found myself doubting everything he ever said to me. He was a liar, a cheater, and a user, after all. And then, *I still slept with him that night.* Was it shock? Fear? Delusion? Primal attraction? I can't tell you anymore.

I did not remain the Other Woman and quietly removed myself from Max's life after that night. But how far did things have to go for me to draw the line?

I was left feeling used, bemused, pitiful, and angry at myself for how everything had unfolded and my behavior in response. The ultimate trap of not using your masculine energy to protect and serve your feminine energy is that you will often blame and judge yourself later. When you are in shock or unconsciously worried about your physical or emotional safety, you will likely struggle to make clear decisions and use your words and actions effectively. If you are aware of your boundaries and needs, feel free to state them up front rather than waiting to see if someone violates a place of safety for you.

Start slowly, one choice at a time, allowing your masculine energy to serve your feminine in small ways, and then grow that energetic service over time. You will become sovereign over your emotional and physical safety with practice. You will learn to say yes when you mean yes, and no when you mean no. You will learn to leave when you don't want to be there. You will take yourself and your emotions more seriously than your date and his. You will become someone who is safe and trustworthy, and therefore you will require the same from your partner. When you balance your masculine and feminine energies, you will experience personal power.

Exercise: Balancing Your Masculine Energy

Here is an exercise to help you notice what your masculine energy is already doing for you and consider one new habit to integrate into your life starting today.

Write down an answer to each of these questions. You may end up with a long list of bullet points or a paragraph or two. Your answer is your own so feel free to add your own flair to your process.

1. How do you serve and protect yourself physically?

   Think: taking care of your body, eating habits, sleep, warmth, exercise, etc.

2. How do you serve and protect yourself energetically?

   Think: having fun, filling your cup, meditation, getting in touch with yourself, etc.

3. How do you serve and protect yourself financially?

   Think: taking care of your material needs, knowing you can get what you need, having a safety net, etc.

4. How do you serve and protect yourself socially?

   Think: knowing how much socialization is the right amount for you, having great friendships, connecting with people and animals in general, etc.

5. How do you serve and protect yourself mentally?

   Think: taking care of your need and desire to learn, grow, create, express yourself, etc.

What is one new thing you can start doing today in each of these categories?

TL;DR

1. Feminine energy is inward-focused. Masculine energy is outward-directed. The highest purpose of masculine energy is to serve feminine energy. Masculine action is intended to support feminine being.

2. Understand that safety and trust are of utmost importance in dating and that you may behave strangely or dysfunctionally when you feel physically or emotionally threatened.

3. Understand that when you are a great seductress, good dates are not a scarce commodity. Permit yourself to let go of people who disregard who you are and what you want. Require better treatment by saying no thank you to people who can't meet you where you are.

4. Notice when you assert your needs and wants with people you're attracted to and when you hide them.

5. Act in service to yourself and see what begins to change in your life.

6. Begin by observing your needs, wants, and emotions and then move to honoring and acting on them.

7. Learn to trust yourself first; you will find that trusting a man to love you and treat you well comes naturally.

CHAPTER 4

SHIFT TO BEING

The first and most fundamental feminine energy shift is from masculine doing to the feminine energy of being. In dating, it can be very easy to slip into the trap of what to do to get someone to like you, to get someone to call you, or to get someone to ask you out. Stop spending energy on what to do. Instead, focus on who you are. How are you doing? What is it you want in connection or a dating relationship? Get connected to yourself and your own being.

One potential challenge for you if you live in mainstream western culture is that we are socialized to value doing over being. Raise your hand if you believe you're a good person when you're checking things off your list and getting things done. You believe that when you are productive, you are worthwhile. You think that you need to achieve a level of activity and output to succeed. You need to work hard to be lovable. You need to do something to prove yourself worthy. You may feel that you're especially good and lovable when doing things for others.

Here's the thing, being in masculine action is awesome. Masculine *doing* energy is incredibly powerful, practical, and to be celebrated. This is not a book about tossing aside your masculine energy and never being active and achievement-oriented again. However, shift out of doing energy for dating and any time you create sexual attraction. Your attractive self is your relaxed self *being* you, unbothered by the masculine energy of *doing*. You will attract the love you want once you focus on your state of *being*.

How To Energetically Attract Your Partner

Your hottest, most attractive self is your relaxed self. Have you noticed that your relaxed self is funny, smart, and interesting enough for other people to enjoy hanging out with you? Do you have at least one friend or family member who enjoys your company? When relaxed, you may notice that you are already lovable and attractive. Bear in mind that being relaxed does not mean lounging on a couch; you can be busy and active in life while remaining relaxed.

When you are in a state of relaxation, who you are is already intriguing and magnetic to your ideal partner. You will come alive when you are deeply rooted in the energy of your own being, connected to who you are and how you feel. You will show up to dating as the Self who knows herself, the self who knows what her nervous system is doing and what she really wants. You will be the part of yourself who is ready to be seen, heard, and connected. This chapter contains several exercises to help you connect to your natural being.

As you practice all the feminine energy shifts in this book, your sexual energy will likely also rise, which will lead to you attracting more interest and romantic offers than you can perhaps currently imagine. One of my favorite testimonials to receive from my group program is when women notice that people begin to see them, hear them, and treat them with more respect and interest when they are in their feminine energy.

When you know how you are being, you will wield incredible relational power.

What I Used To Do

After working as a nanny in Germany, I realized I never wanted to be an unskilled laborer again. So I returned to the pine trees of Oregon for college. Elias and I met in an upper-level German class during my first quarter of freshman year. I was in the class because I had literally talked my way into it by speaking German to the professor. I hadn't completed the prerequisite grammar classes to be there; I had simply learned the language the way Germans do, by living in Germany and speaking the language all day, every day. I didn't know why the grammar worked the way it did. I just knew how to use it, mostly.

But from the moment I sat down in class the first day, I did not quite feel I had earned the right to be there. I felt that the other students knew more than I did and had more of a right to be there than I did. They were also several years older, well-seasoned college and graduate students.

Elias and I were paired up for a partner discussion about the Mozart opera *The Abduction From The Seraglio*. We did not talk about the opera for long. He was very interested in the fact that I had lived in Germany, and I was fascinated by his life story. He had lived a fast and furious life, with lots of extreme sports and travel. Then he had been in a motorcycle accident a few years before, sustained a severe brain injury, and lost four months of memory. Consequently, he continued to suffer from a type of short-term memory loss. He was exciting. Did I mention he was extremely attractive? I spoke better German than he did, but he understood the syntax and rules behind the grammar.

We started a ritual of walking home from class together, as we lived on the same side of the university campus. We walked and talked about healing, travel, and adrenaline-inducing sports and activities. All I could think about was what I could *do* to get him to like me more. What could I *do* to get him to ask me out? What could I *do* to be his girlfriend? Wondering what to do made me nervous. It made me uncertain about what I *was* doing. So here's the whole enchilada of what I was doing: getting to know someone attractive.

All you are doing when you are dating is getting to know someone you find romantically and/or sexually attractive. There I was, getting to know someone sexy and fun, and all I could think about was what else

I should be doing to get him to want me. And then I criticized myself for not doing it right when he didn't do exactly what I secretly wanted.

Eventually, our class ended, and he did ask me out. A huge surge of nerves and excitement on my end accompanied every text exchange. I was constantly worried about what to say and do about his texts. How long should I wait till I reply? What kind of response would be best? Witty? Matter-of-fact? Something that made him think? A mix of all three?

We went to see a late-night movie on Tuesday. We were the only ones in the theater, and so we made out at least half of the film. I didn't go home with him. I didn't *do* first-date sleepovers. I had learned that withholding sex was the best way to get a man to want you for a real relationship. I wanted the relationship. The nervousness in texting and interacting with him did not subside with time and inconsistent text contact. Even though he had asked me out, taken me out, and made out with me, I still felt insecure about whether he liked me.

I didn't know how to talk to him, but I did believe that there was something I could *do* to make him really want me. He made me dinner at his house and tried to get me to sleep with him. I said *no* because I wanted to be perceived as a girl who was hard to get and make it obvious that I didn't just sleep with anyone after two dates. I said no to prove that I was girlfriend material, but I didn't mention to him that I wanted a relationship. I didn't want to appear needy or desperate.

I did not say, "I'm really looking for a serious relationship," or even, "I'd rather wait until we know each other better before taking that step." Instead, I tried to figure out what I needed to *do* to be cool, hard to get, and wanted. After a month and four dates, I said yes to sex. It seemed like the right thing to do to bring the relationship to the next level. Maybe then he would know if he really wanted me.

The following day at 5:45 a.m., he drove me home because he needed to go to the gym. He was disciplined about going every day, he said. Although I wanted to sleep in, cuddle, and maybe have more sex, I did not protest our pre-dawn separation nor express my wish for more intimacy. I said, "no problem," and tried hard not to feel devalued, discarded, and unfulfilled.

After sex, I perceived Elias as pulling away, texting less often, and expressing less interest. I wasn't sure what to *do* about it. I hung onto the connection, accepting offers to hang out, but becoming more of a phantom of myself with him, expressing less and less of what I wanted, thought, and who I was. We only had dates at his house after that. I watched him flirt with his roommate in front of me while I observed from the sidelines, giggling when it seemed appropriate. How do people go from dating to relationships? I asked myself. What do they *do*?

Two weeks went by, and he didn't contact me at all. Likewise, I didn't reach out to him. Mirroring someone else's behavior instead of relying on my own desire seemed like the best strategy at the time. Then a Facebook post told me that Elias was in a relationship with a different woman.

I went to her profile. She looked like me but with a cuter nose, bluer eyes, blonder, smoother hair, and a fitter body. She was also doing the splits in half of her pictures—a gymnast. There was nothing I could *do* to be better than that.

The heartbreak was significantly softer than with Martin, but it still stung. I was still the unwanted leftover girl. I finished second. I was not The One he chose.

You may have been in similar situations before, where you tried to act a certain way or do something to get someone to notice you, want you, ask you out, or fall in love with you. Unfortunately, these strategies rarely work the way you wish they would. The most powerful thing you can do to create more attraction in dating is to shift into the feminine energy state of being.

Imagine if I had noticed how I was being when Elias and I met. Imagine if I had seen all my insecurities and feelings of unworthiness and then addressed those insecurities. I might have realized I was amazing and shifted my energy around him. What do you want to bet that I was *being* insecure and *behaving* unworthily whenever I was around him?

It does not matter when or how often you text or communicate, whether you wear this dress or that on a date, what you do for a living, or which exact date you sleep together or have your first kiss. In every case, you need to shift all your focus to who *you* are being. Whenever you catch yourself in a tailspin of anxiety around whether you are dating "correctly" in order to get what you want from a man, shift your focus to how *you* are being.

How Men Fall In Love

Evolutionary biology (the study of mating and procreating) theories suggest that men fall in love with personality traits and how they feel when they're with you. Alternately, women fall in love with competence, skill, and demonstration of ability. You are tapping into this distinction by living into the feminine energy of being - you are making space for a masculine-energy man to fall in love with who you are.

Because I was attracted to competence and skill, for a long time, I tried to convince the men I dated how competent I was and how many skills I had. For example, with Elias, I tried to prove to him how intelligent I was; I had the urge to show him how good I was at cooking and how much great girlfriend potential I had.

"Proving energy" is not seductive to men. Whenever you are tempted to prove your lovability, you have moved into masculine doing energy, dampening attraction potential. Additionally, no specific strategic action you can take will fundamentally change a man's feelings for you. What will change their feelings is a shift to feminine energy, transforming your presence around them and creating a mind-blowing emotional connection with them. You will learn all of this through the course of this book.

It is your energetic being that the masculine falls in love with. The way your spirit pours out of you or how you sit quietly waiting for the bus. It is how sassy you get when you order drinks at the bar or if you silently read the menu start-to-finish before deciding on food. It's in how you focus your attention on him during the date and how you live in your body. It is whether or not you get up first to dance at a wedding or how you react when the sun hits your eyes.

It is not what sports you do or don't watch, what career you may or not be successful at, or whether you have won any awards. You can try to impress a man with your talent and knowledge, but it will not make a difference in his level of desire for you. He does not fall in love with exterior details. He may admire and want to sleep with a woman for her beauty but even that isn't what fills him with the desire to be with her, and only her, fully and completely.

Masquerading Masculine Energy

Here's one more thing I want to emphasize. Cooking, cleaning, and raising children are all outward energy activities - yes, expressions of masculine energy. You will likely feel less sexual energy while doing these activities. And while a man may appreciate, enjoy, or even think he needs the support of all your hard work, the energy between you when you offer him these services will not be pure sexual attraction. I recommend putting some time and space at the beginning of any relationship seduction before you add these activities to your dating connection.

When doing these activities are part of who you are, they will be present in your dating life without you having to work them in or prove them. For example, I genuinely love hanging out with children, which means I have a lot of fun and playful energy. I light up when I see children. I didn't need to engineer situations for men to see me interact with kids. I didn't need to prove I would make a good mother by showing or explaining my childcare skills. I am also highly empathic, which means I am a great listener and gentle with people's emotions. When I shifted my focus to *being*, the playful and empathic parts of myself showed up on dates naturally. I never needed to make an effort to work in stories that drew attention to my external qualities or abilities and proved I was a catch. Those ways of being are who I am already.

Cook for your date only if you love cooking, and it is an authentic way you express love. Shift away from any activity that has a flavor of "should," "need to prove," or "have to do this" to get attention or love.

A word that often shows up in descriptions of the feminine is *nurturing*. Understand that this does not mean taking care of everyone's needs, which is a masculine energy act of *doing*. Feminine nurture means that your presence is nurturing. You support others by being your true, loving self. A female body nurtures new human life by simply being alive - sleeping, eating, and caring for her own body. Feminine nurturing is about how you are, not what you do for others.

Being attractive, seductive, and wanted is not about how much you work and do. Anytime, and I mean anytime at all, that you feel tempted to do something or fix something in a dating connection, shift your focus to your own being first.

Here are actions you may consider taking when you want him to notice or fall in love with you:

- Texting him to make sure he's thinking of you
- Texting him a check-in but hoping he'll ask you out
- Cooking for him
- Taking care of him
- Taking care of his house
- Acting as his therapist
- Acting as his nurse
- Proving to him that you are good with children
- Proving to him you are good in bed

Here's the thing, while these actions can all be supportive partner behavior and integrated into a long-term relationship, they are not part of building initial sexy attraction. Feminine seduction is not about what you DO for a man.

Here are some feminine things you can lean into: anything that starts with BEING (these include all character/emotional traits).

Being joyful

Being furious

Being fun

Being well

Once you know how you are and can be with your authentic self, everything else falls into place.

Shift To Being

You want to shift away from activities you do because it will get them to want you, like texting or agreeing to meet them somewhere inconvenient. And you want to shift into the energy of a calm nervous system. Your nervous system is a complex network of nerves connected to your brain and spinal cord. It manages the messages between your brain and body, ruling many automatic emotions and physical responses. Becoming a great seductress is about reclaiming nervous system sovereignty, so you can remain calm, creative, and relational as much as possible. Your calm nervous system state is that relaxed self we talked about earlier. It is you with no or low levels of stress or anxiety. Stress and excitement at low levels create attraction, but stress, in abundance, is an attraction killer. That being said, getting a handle on the stress you feel in dating is often easier said than done.

Likely, when you meet someone super attractive, your ability to communicate directly or coherently goes out the window. You might be tempted to flip out when someone you like stops messaging you on a dating app. You might feel the urge to spend a few days watching television and eating chocolate, send them a scathing message, or delete and block them. When you feel like you're losing control in a relationship, you are likely to lash out or shrink back. These things probably happen to you automatically, and your reaction to whomever you were talking to, dating, or crushing on likely feels involuntary. You often are not thinking neutrally, as in, *hey, I just matched with this guy two weeks ago. His behavior doesn't affect my life in any significant way.* Or maybe after a few weeks of dating, *I thought this guy was a catch, but he's still emotionally involved with his ex. Thank you, next.* When your nervous system senses physical or emotional danger, like rejection, neglect, or being misunderstood, it transmits a message through your body to protect. Your automatic protection response may or may not match the gravity of the situation. It may not actually support your desired outcome. For example, I wanted to be closer to Elias, but my actions were things like withholding sex or waiting entire days to text him back to prove to him that I had a full life.

Your personal response to dating stress is part of you, but the sexy part of you that I recommend you bring to the seduction phase of dating is your regulated nervous system self. The relaxed you. The fastest way back to this state of being is through attention to your breath. Use the following exercise to breathe intentionally whenever dating feels challenging. It will calm and reset your nervous system and get you out of your unhelpful emotions and automatic responses.

Exercise: Breathe

Many of us in modern times are not breathing to our fullest capacity.

If it's safe to do so, complete this exercise with your eyes closed. This will help you notice your inner experience more effectively. Sit up straight so that your rib cage opens up and gives your lungs plenty of room. Breathe in deeply and exhale all of it. Notice your body. Breathe in once more and relax your stomach. Feel your gut fill up as you breathe. Breathe in and relax your shoulders. Breathe out, relax, or even wiggle your hips and toes. Inhale and exhale and notice how you are. Keep breathing fully and completely.

Let yourself be however you are without judgment or bullying yourself about how you "should be" right now. You are building up your power to *be*.

Use this simple breathing technique whenever you are tempted to figure out what to do, say, or change about a dating relationship. Just be without self-judgment for a moment and breathe. When you're freaking out because a hottie just glanced at you as he walked by… Breathe.

When someone attractive speaks to you, and you mutter something not clever that maybe didn't even make sense in the context… breathe. When you're not getting any matches on online dating sites… Breathe. When you're getting too many matches, just breathe. Being you is not a static state. You are not fixed in time, nor even fixed to an identity, a personality, a way of expressing yourself, or a way of being.

Your emotions change—your body changes. Your priorities change. Your thoughts change. There isn't a *you* that is more or less you than you are right now. For dating, we're interested in engaging the you that knows you are magnetic, desirable, and worthy of love. The part of you that is relaxed, connected to yourself, and able to connect genuinely to others.

The easiest access to this state of being that I know is through your breath. It chills you out and cuts through all the noise in your head about how you're not enough and what you should be doing.

As I did with Elias, you can show up to dating with your scarred and scared Self, the Self that isn't sure you're worth it and feels the need to do something to prove, the Self that doesn't yet know how to make herself safe, or assert her wants and needs. Or you can show up in your power.

You can show up embodied. You can be confident, sensual, mysterious, or whatever else you want to be in a romance. You can know yourself and show up as that self. You don't have to know her today. What you are doing in reading this book is cultivating awareness of your body, energy, and power. You are allowed to take time and practice to become a great seductress. First, just breathe and be.

First Impressions

Attraction begins when someone notices *something about you*. Therefore, the first step to becoming a powerful seductress is being noticed. This doesn't necessarily mean a giant spotlight shines down on you from the sky or that all eyes land on you when you walk into a room. It simply means there's something about you that a romantic potential notices as a first impression. You don't need to achieve your ideal weight and then don a red glitter dress and get followed around by paparazzi to be seen by the right person for you. You only need a special *something* in your presence that clicks in your someone's mind. Some intrigue. A little double-take.

Aside from having a relaxed nervous system, the best way to attract attention in dating is by being your full self. All of you! Your perfect love match is someone who is compatible with who you truly are. The more you express yourself in life and dating, the closer you will be to creating a lasting relationship. So breathe more, and then start to get curious about who you are and how you can express more of your true self in your life.

I continued to shrink myself with Elias. At the beginning of our connection, I showed up as an intriguing bilingual world traveler who readily discussed Mozart arias. By the end, I was a girl fake-giggling on a kitchen stool while he swatted his roommate's butt with a hand towel.

Being honest about who you are can feel scary. The potential for rejection feels real because if someone doesn't want you, they have rejected the real you. But why be in a relationship with someone incompatible with who you really are? What makes you want to stay with someone who is a bad fit for you? When you trust yourself as a great seductress, you will feel more confident about saying no to bad matches.

How can you bring more of yourself to dating? Hint: We've already looked at several ways, specifically, getting in touch with your desires and knowing what you want to experience in dating. Complete the exercises at the end of this chapter for further insight on how to express more of yourself in your love life.

Intrigue and Invitation

If the idea of being all of you has you feeling wobbly because you believe you are too much or not enough in dating, Intrigue and Invitation Balance is a useful tool for first impressions and first dates. Balancing Intrigue and Invitation is a little trick I used for myself during initial dating conversations. I struggled to find the right mix of sharing about myself and listening to romantic potential. I am a great listener, but when I get going, I can talk a lot and sometimes "overshare." Other times, I sat silently and listened to men monologue about their lives and thoughts. I tended to be either too quiet or spill my whole life story right away. As a result, I experienced being too much *and* not enough of myself on dates.

A great seductress is both a warm invitation and profoundly intriguing. Most of us fall to one side or the other in terms of being inviting (outgoing and/or friendly) or intriguing (shy and/or cool). You likely know which side of the spectrum you tend to fall in romantic situations.

You do not need to change how you are to be sexy and wanted, but becoming aware of your intrigue and invitation balance can help you feel empowered in dating conversations.

If you are so open you tend to overshare, try on *intrigue* for size. Play around with your mysterious side. Rather than telling your date your whole life story in the first two hours you meet, practice holding the energy of "I have a little secret that I just might tell you." Play a game with yourself. You don't share any stories about "x" in your life. You can also purposefully schedule your life so phone calls and first dates don't last more than two hours. This gives your match time to get to know you outside of "stories" that come up when you get too excited or comfortable and can't keep track of whether you're charming or overwhelming your date.

For full transparency, I completely blew the two-hour rule on my first date with my husband. Nevertheless, I consider our seduction phase flawless, so remember the wise words of Matthew Hussey, world-renowned dating coach, "it's hard to screw up the right thing." You don't need to straight-jacket yourself into some perceived perfect balance of being inviting and intriguing. You simply want to be aware of how you're showing up and who you're being with new connections.

If you tend to be shy or hold back with new people, you're in luck; you are naturally intriguing. To balance with an invitation, engage your empathy muscle. You don't need to become the life of the party; you just need to be warm enough to show a date that you care about things, so they can imagine that someday you will care about them. Even a small display of empathy and warmth will do it. This looks like a smile, a laugh, or an emotional acknowledgment of something they say. You can say something like, "that sounds tough," when they talk about their average work day, or "Wow, you would be a great sommelier," when they list the traits of their favorite wine.

Balancing intrigue and invitation will give you an edge during any seduction because it will help you create an emotional connection with less anxiety. Both oversharing and withholding yourself from new people are anxiety-driven responses. Using this tool will help you if you naturally tend to overpower others or shrink socially when nervous. And don't forget to keep breathing.

Exercise: You As A Great Seductress

Highly seductive people vary greatly in size, shape, style, personality, and habits, but they all have one thing in common: whoever they are, they are wholeheartedly committed to being themselves. We looked at a few examples of great seductresses in Chapter 1. Now it's time to explore your personal flavor of great seductress. Who are you and how can you bring more of yourself to dating?

Begin to think about how you tend to your energy, especially your passionate energy. Get out a pen and paper and write out the answers to these questions.

1. What lights me up?

2. What parts of myself have I been ignoring?

3. What makes me beautiful?

4. How does the way I dress and adorn my body make me feel? Think about hair, piercings, tattoos, and makeup as well.

5. What parts of myself have I been highlighting in dating? What parts of myself would I like to bring forward in romance?

6. What is possible in my life if I feel energetically nourished, know myself, feel great, and match my outer appearance to honor the inner experience of being myself?

Once I had solidly devoted myself to feminine energy, I chose to go back to vocal school and learned more about singing. It was a craft I had spent a lot of time honing in childhood because I loved it more than anything, but because people told me over and over that I couldn't earn real money with it, I abandoned the study and practice of voice after college.

Now I practice it, invest in it, and do it because I love music at the core of my being, and using my voice is a huge part of maintaining positive and balanced energy for me. When it comes to supporting your life energy, look beyond monetary return on investment when making decisions. Devote time, energy, and potentially money to the parts of you that are important. It is *never* too late to reclaim your passions, find new ones, or invest time, energy, or money in things that revitalize your energy, such as rest, spa treatments, or exercise.

That inner transformation in value also took place outside me in my personal style. Previously I had relied on magazines, models, and what was available in mainstream stores to determine my wardrobe. I let the outer world decide how I dressed. Shopping for clothes was difficult for me. Outfits that looked great on mannequins looked awkward on me. I didn't fit into pants. I felt I had poor taste and couldn't put garments together well. When I saw myself in pictures, I never looked the way I imagined.

At the beginning of my feminine seduction journey, I spent many hours poring over articles on dressing different body shapes and skin tones and how to think about fabrics. I followed several YouTube stylists and wardrobe curators to learn how different clothing cuts and colors affected my appearance. I studied how to dress my own body shape (petite, round-limbed, pear). Finally, I settled on creating a capsule wardrobe of clothing that fits me, accentuates my favorite features, balances the shapes of my body, and compliments my skin tone. My style discovery took about a year to accomplish and is ever-evolving. I can now be intentional about how I dress in a way that honors who I am and how I feel on a particular day. I dress for myself. I am essentially unconcerned about how the way I dress affects others.

Exercise: Create a *Being* Practice for Dating

This is the only MUST-DO exercise in this chapter. Choose and implement a daily practice around being.

Here are several suggestions, but it's not an exhaustive list. I recommend picking just one or two for starters to keep it simple. Eventually, you may incorporate many of them into your life.

1. Take five deep breaths every morning and evening.

2. Make a list of ways you want to be in dating (kind, fun, energetic, etc.) and practice bringing them into your daily life now.

3. Make a list of powerful things you are (caring, wise, funny, regal, etc.), and keep it somewhere you will see regularly.

4. Breathe intentionally before making any dating decisions or moves.

5. Connect with your breath when standing in any line.

6. Connect with your breath whenever you get the urge to prove something to someone.

7. Take up some form of yoga or meditation.

8. Stop initiating contact from dates (I recommend this if you are currently the primary instigator).

9. When offering help, double-check your service tendency - are you doing things for others out of a sense of obligation or a true sense of joy in taking care of them?

10. Brainstorm ways to bring more of your authentic self to different areas of your life: family, career, love, etc.

TL;DR

1. Being is the feminine energy opposite the masculine energy of doing.

2. At all times during the seduction phase of dating and anytime you want to create sexual attraction, shift your focus from doing to your being.

3. Generally speaking, men fall in love with your being and how they feel when near you. Women fall in love with competence and demonstrations of ability (think romantic gestures).

4. There is no specific strategic action you can take that will fundamentally change a masculine person's feelings for you.

5. During seduction, remain in the category of lover, rather than mom, therapist, nurse, caretaker, housecleaner, cook, or childcare provider.

6. You have the power to shift back to your least-activated self at any point by using your breath.

7. Being all of yourself on dates is the best way to find a perfect-fit match, but if you tend to stress out, get overexcited, or shut down in the face of romance, use Invitation/Intrigue Balance to get back on track.

8. Cultivate your presence.

CHAPTER 5

SHIFT TO RECEIVING

Feminine energy is the energy of receiving, which is polarized by masculine giving. For the ultimate experience of the feminine and the juiciest attraction to the masculine, focus on what you are receiving in romance. Take the focus off what you give.

What does it feel like to receive his presence, attention, words, and actions? In dating, how much attention can you bear to receive? How much affection, time, and effort can you take? We all have a limit to how much love we believe we can receive. Where is your receiving limit? The more you can *receive* attention, admiration, and love, the more attractive you will become. When you are adept at receiving, people want to give you more. People love to give love, and the man who is ready to create a loving relationship with you will love giving love to you.

Commitment Isn't Feeling Wanted

Dating in college was not rewarding for me. I endured a couple of odd hookups at parties and attempts to date friends of my friends. I reached senior year with the same feelings of rejection and failure I faced with Martin, Max, and Elias.

I met Austin at my coworker's party. My coworker was cool, and I knew she had cool friends, so I went, although I was tired and didn't want to party. I was still living life from a deep sense of obligation rather than joy or my natural energy of feminine being. I arrived late, didn't drink, and left early.

Just before I left, I came across her very drunk friend, Austin, in the kitchen. He flirted with me, and although I didn't flirt back, he asked me for my number. No one had ever asked me for my number at a party before, so I was slightly in shock. I put my number in his phone. He asked me out in a text the next day.

This is what it's like to be a normal girl, I thought. Had I made it to the dating Olympics? Someone had asked me out directly without any trickery or months of lead-up. I accepted the date.

Austin and I went to a burger joint and had a fine time. He was attractive in a way that wasn't my usual type, with light brown hair and big brown eyes that gave off sweetness rather than mystery. He was goofy and kind. I was working very hard to get on board the "nice guy" ship. At the time, it was a cultural norm to make fun of women for wanting "bad boys" and then complaining about mistreatment. I wanted to stop being one of those women.

I had not yet read about the very intelligent hormones and biology that encourage women to desire warrior energy. We are biologically compelled to seek a man willing to use aggression to protect us but with the self-mastery to never use it against us. Often, however, men are not taught the self-mastery of channeling their testosterone into purposeful aggression, nor the concept of masculine energy serving feminine energy. This leads to aggressive masculine men without a meaningful cause to fight for.

I had forced myself to get on the "nice guy boat" twice to save myself from my undesired singlehood. I had a few dates and kisses with respectable men I had to try hard to want and failed. Your body and heart know what they like, and when you relax into your being, you will have access to natural, sexy attraction. Forcing or hoping for eventual attraction despite a lack of interest is a useless dating strategy.

Austin was different from the other nice guys. He was easy to be with and funny but with a quiet shroud of sadness around him. He smelled of oatmeal, vegetable soup, and something slightly acidic. It intrigued me. Our first date was comfortable and laid back. We each paid for our own meals in a friendly and egalitarian way. I didn't know about receiving from the masculine, so I paid no attention to what I was offered in terms of love, effort, or meals.

Our second date was watching a movie on a couch where I was housesitting. We ended the night by making out. Our attraction was not exceptionally heated - perhaps on either side. He admitted he had dated and then remained friends with my coworker and been attracted to another friend in their common friend group. I tried hard to shake the idea that I was just a woman who had come along and not said *no* to him. I had no idea the polarity of giving and receiving could help ignite our attraction. But he didn't repulse me as a man, which was usually where my endeavors to date people I wasn't strongly attracted to ended. I didn't know what I wanted, so I didn't know to set a higher bar.

After a month of talking and hanging out, we slept together, as one month to bed was my rule at the time. I was honest with him about my medical condition and the pain I usually experienced during sex. This time, the pain was tolerable. He asked me to be his girlfriend. There was something that felt very young about the word *girlfriend*, but I shrugged it off. The meaning of the question was exactly what I wanted. Commitment. Being chosen.

Only commitment didn't feel like I imagined. I didn't feel madly in love. I didn't feel as intoxicated as I had with Martin. Commitment with him didn't feel like he was saying, "you, and only you, are The One I want." It felt anti-climactic. Different than I had imagined love, attachment, and commitment. I didn't know what these felt like; I just felt I was falling short. I was unable to receive the full scope of the love and commitment I wanted. I was constantly on the lookout for signs that Austin wasn't attracted to me.

His bid for commitment was, in fact, not enough to make me feel wanted. There was little sexual tension in our connection because I was still uncomfortable flirting. We had sex on Wednesdays when my roommate was at work. He only liked American food, and I preferred food from around the world. He loved movies, and I preferred social activities and going out. We watched movies at home on the couch, and we talked. He was funny and charming and self-taught in many subjects. He was engaged with the world. I was interested in his personality but bored by our relationship. I did not know about creating emotional connection, and he did not ask the kinds of questions that got to the depths of who I was. Deep down, beneath our jokes and regular hangouts, I felt unseen, unheard, and unimportant.

Three months in, we went out with his group of friends. It was a dark arcade bar with lots of noise and flashing lights. He barely spoke to me or paid me much attention, but I felt glad to be there with someone. For the first time in my life, I was part of a group with my person instead of alone. Watching him interact with other people, I noticed a habit he had when speaking to others, including myself. He never met people's eyes when speaking to them, though direct eye contact during communication is a cultural norm for white Americans.

When we were alone together for a moment, I asked him if he was on the autism spectrum. I intended it as an innocent question. My personal relationship with autism was and is that it is one way for the brain to process - not necessarily better or worse than anyone else's way of processing. For me, it was evident that he was a highly capable adult. Still, I thought it would explain some of his habits, specifically, the lack of curiosity about me as an emotional person and avoiding people's eyes when speaking. However, he felt insulted and became incredibly angry.

"How could you say that?" He demanded, "You have no tact."

And the fun of the night out was over for us.

It was the first time a man had directly given me negative feedback about myself in a relationship. I juggled self-soothing and tending to the relationship. I tried to apologize and explain my view of autism, but the damage was done. His view was different. We drove in silence back to my apartment and quietly got into bed.

"I'm sorry," I said again, rolling over to look at him.

What came out of his mouth next was not what I expected. He stared up at the ceiling and told me stories from his childhood, stories of a father in prison, and the legacy of abuse in his past. He had been told that he was a piece of shit many times as a child and had created the instinct to hide from his father. He never said, "and that's why I don't look people directly in the face," but I understood. Then I was still sorry, but for different reasons.

It was the first time real emotional intimacy had come up in our relationship, three months in. What had been keeping us together before? Mutual loneliness? Preferring to be together rather than apart?

At the three-month mark, time with him started to drag. We did not create further emotional intimacy between us. We continued to have sex on Wednesdays and watch movies on the weekends. I became outright resentful of how much time we spent on the couch and how unwilling he was to go out. He didn't have a job and didn't feel he had the money. I began to gain weight very quickly, a common sign of deep-rooted unhappiness for me.

We did not give each other up, but neither of us was satisfied, and time kept running. Finally, I told him we *had* to go out and I would just pay for everything. I believed this was how I could get what I wanted.

We went out, and I paid, but he sulked the entire evening. Therefore we did not have the fun and enlivening time I imagined we would. We sat there in a crowded bar we both claimed to like. With cheerful banter all around us, we said almost nothing to each other. I sipped my drink in defeat.

This is depressing, I thought to myself. I had *given* the money for the night out and *done* what I needed to be done to create the date I wanted. I told him we were going out, made the plan, and executed it. There I was, on the date I'd been craving for months, but I wasn't having the experience of relationship that I wanted. I had actually forced him on a date and tried to control our intimacy. A month later, I told him it wasn't working, and we had to break up.

"Okay," he said hesitantly and quietly.

I started to cry.

Then, he switched roles and comforted me, saying, "We can still be friends,"

"For real?" I choked out.

"Yes, of course," he assured me.

We said goodbye, but after a brief text exchange a week later, we never spoke again. Commitment and time in a relationship mean nothing without intimacy. You must be able to receive attention, love, and commitment in order to feel fulfilled by the level of relationship you desire. However, commitment is not synonymous with feeling wanted. And, if you are unaware of what you are receiving in a relationship, it's easy to end up in an unfulfilling situation. If you are unable to receive, a masculine person will feel he isn't able to give to you. When you cannot shift into receiving, your connection will suffer.

How to Receive and Decline

Becoming skilled at receiving doesn't just create a juicy feminine aura around you; it prepares you for receiving support in the relationship big leagues. The first step in skilled receiving is becoming aware of what you want.

Remember your deepest desire from Chapter 1? That exercise was an introduction to getting in touch with all your desires. During seduction, you want to be deeply in touch with what you desire at all times. Accept what you wish to and decline what you don't. Do you *want* to talk on the phone with an online dating match tonight? Do you *want* to go to that restaurant? Do you *want* to go to his house or do you prefer somewhere public? It will make receiving safer if you feel comfortable saying no when you don't want something.

As a great seductress, you want to be grounded in your desires so you know when to receive and when to say no thank you. For some of you, this will be harder than for others. Sometimes it takes practice to start being aware of what you want. Many of us have been socialized to think about what other people want before considering our own desire. Often, people like me with deeply internalized self-sufficiency and unworthiness stories struggle with receiving. If you believe you should be able to do things by yourself, it will be challenging to receive. If you think that when people give you something, pay for you, or take care of you, it means you owe them in return or that you are weak, it will be difficult to feel empowered when you receive. If you are not sure you deserve what you want or are worthy of what you want, you may even reject it when it is offered directly to you.

To start out, you don't have to believe you are worthy of what you want. You can act like it. Fake it until you make it. Act like you are worth it. If receiving from men or dates is truly difficult for you, start small in other areas of your life. When someone offers to get you a coffee, accept. Take a moment to feel receptive as you hold the warm coffee cup between your hands. Say thank you. When someone compliments you, accept their words. Feel the compliment. Say thank you. When someone offers to help you fix something you don't want to fix yourself, accept. Receive the support. Say thank you.

If you do not want what is offered, say no thank you. It is that simple, even if it isn't easy. If you ever feel uncertain during the dating process, it's usually a sign you have been offered something you don't want. Breathe. Check in with your body about what is going on. What part of the situation are you uncomfortable with? What can you ask for or say no to that will make the situation work for you? I still use this simple process today when I receive offers or invitations that make me uncomfortable. In dating, declining purposefully is an essential tool. The more you practice breathing, checking in, and speaking up for what you need, the more natural it will feel. Soon, you'll be receiving on dates like an absolute pro. A great seductress doesn't accept offers, gifts, or lovers she doesn't want, and you won't either.

Receptivity On Dates

How to apply receptivity directly in dating? Look for ways to receive masculine presence, attention, affection, and support. At all times during the seduction phase, ask yourself, "what am I receiving from this man right now?" Allow him to come up with discussion topics in dating app chats. Receive his thought process and personality. Consider that you want to be in a relationship with someone who communicates well with you.

Allow him to open doors, carry umbrellas, and hold things for you. Receive his acts of service. Consider that you want to be in a relationship with someone who is able to think of your needs as well as his own. Unless he says no thank you, allow him to pay for the date. Receive his display of financial capacity *and* observe his relationships with money and generosity. A man will feel more attracted to you when he gives to you.

Allowing men to pay for dates was incredibly difficult for me at first, but I was converted when I noticed that men who paid the check smiled bigger at my thank you and cared more about our time together. They always wanted to see me again. Why is this? Masculine people often relate to the elements of their world as investments. Observe where he invests his time, energy, and money, and allow it to be you. During this process, he develops more attraction, feelings, and attachment to you.

Allow him to give to you in bed. Receive his pleasure. Consider having a non-transactional relationship with love and sex, meaning a relationship where nothing is owed, and everything is desired. On that note, know that you *never* owe anyone your body or time. You do not owe someone sex because they bought you dinner. You do not need to see them again because they admitted something to you they usually keep secret. You do not need to give just because you received. In the end, relationships are qualitative, not quantitative, even when money is involved. Receptivity is about creating relationships, not debts. Now, one more time for the people in the back, you *never* owe someone your body or time.

If you ever feel uncertain about receiving during a conversation or a date, pause, lean back on your heels or in your chair, and breathe into your belly. Reset your breath and then move forward. You will likely find that your date has already "fixed" the issue during your pause, or you will feel certain you know your answer.

Also, understand that when a man doesn't feel he has much to give you mentally, materially, or spiritually, he will likely not commit to you, or he will commit *noncommittally*. He may be flakey with you, need breaks or "space" away from you, or talk about marriage but never seriously with you. This is not because he doesn't like you or want you at all. It's because he doesn't feel connected to his masculine power to give yet. It is not your fault or even an indication of how much he cares about you. He can be totally smitten and still not want to commit.

When you are a great seductress, you will not mind because you will know that there are plenty of great men out there who will be attracted to you and ready to give love to you freely and effortlessly at the level you desire. However, your side of the bargain is to be ready to receive the love you desire.

Masculine Purpose

Masculine energy desires purpose.

Masculine people almost always prefer purposeful activities and lives.

I used to be bitter about what I perceived as a male tendency only to help women when they wanted something from them or to be strategically useful when they had something to gain from an activity and suspiciously absent when helping out wasn't for their personal benefit.

Welp. As you can imagine, that was a disempowering story that did not gain me much support from men.

By understanding that direct, outward-moving masculine energy prefers purpose, I let go of all that bitterness and even allowed men and people, in general, to help me out. It is often tricky for people with unbalanced masculine energy to accept support from other people. Various fears bottled me up, thinking that asking for or accepting help meant that other people saw me as needy, that I wouldn't get the support I actually craved, or that someone else would do it wrong. Underneath those anxieties were all my fears that I wasn't worth supporting and that needing others made me weak.

In the end, it wasn't a huge effort to reprogram my mind, heal all my fears, or transform my life. I simply started allowing others to experience purpose by being in my life. I allowed friends to support me when I was having a bad day. I allowed strangers to open doors for me when entering shops. I allowed men to advise me about my car, hold objects for me while I shuffled around in my purse, and pay for dates.

Letting your date help you do something is a powerful way to create rapport with a masculine energy person and to see how they respond to supporting you. It communicates to the other person that you trust them and value their effort. It lets them know that not only do you think they're sexy and interesting, you think they're good at doing things. Of course, it doesn't hurt to say thank you after either, making them feel seen and valued.

If you want to end up with a man who understands his energetic sovereignty and responsibility in the relationship, you must be able to accept support. A man who doesn't need reminders to take out the trash and who is generally engaged in being with you and perhaps being the father of your children or dogs is a man who steps up. This man is connected to a sense of purpose.

A great seductress allows masculine people to find purpose in being with her, which means not only allowing support from him but also asking for support when appropriate.

Irresistibly Receptive

The most charming and irresistible way to receive in dating and life is to accept graciously. Say thank you authentically and be specific about what you received. "Thank you for this ice cream. It's exactly what I wanted." "Thank you for this evening. I haven't had this much fun on a date in a long time."

When you thank someone for their gesture, words, or effort, you make their gift meaningful. If you grew up in a capitalist culture, you likely learned that *everything given has a price,* and if you grew up in a patriarchal society, you learned that *to give is better than to receive.* These attitudes can create all kinds of fear and anxiety around receiving, particularly around receiving from men during dating. You may have learned that when you accept something, you owe something tangible in return. Sometimes women feel it is dangerous to receive from men because then you owe them yourself: your body, your time, and your love.

If you are someone with a lot of fear around receiving, and the idea of graciously receiving from men sounds tricky, I invite you to consider this reframe. What if giving and receiving isn't a commodity transaction that requires repayment but a relational transaction that creates a connection? That means that the acts of giving and receiving in dating are meant to create relationships, not debts. You will begin to experience much more fun, relaxation, and connection in dating, and likely in your entire life with this reframe. In addition, you will start to see and experience the power of the feminine energy of receiving.

What if receiving from someone is a gift for them? What if listening to someone is a gift they have been craving? What if allowing them to demonstrate or use a skill or competence enables them to connect to their sense of life purpose? What if receiving from someone means that you value them more? What if receiving from someone gives them the gift of relationship? Begin to unwind your tit-for-tat view of receiving, so that you don't owe goods or services for something given. Connection is also a gift you are already offering. Remember the gift of connection, and then receive graciously when you like what is given.

If you start paying attention when you receive graciously, you will see the aftermath of your gratitude: your dates' eyes will shine when you thank them. Giving to someone who can receive well feels good, and men will love giving to you when you respond with genuine gratitude. Your acknowledgment and gracious receptivity are gifts to him. They create a connection between you. Additionally, when a man gives, he is connected to his masculine energy, which is another gift to him. He gets to tap into his own sexual power. Giving and receiving can be a connection tool rather than a value-based transaction.

Another simple way to shift your *being* energy is to start taking notice of everything you receive throughout your everyday life and say thank you as often as you can to people around you. Even when you're not chatting with a potential match or on a date, these moments of receptivity and gratitude can shift your overall mood and life energy.

Exercise: Practice Receiving Love

My favorite way to practice receiving love is through the 5 Love Languages, as identified by Gary Chapman. They help you receive in exactly the right areas to sustain attraction and long-term love.

1. Physical Touch
2. Words of Affirmation
3. Receiving Gifts
4. Acts of Service
5. Quality Time

Each of these categories is a way to give or receive love, and different people have different ways of feeling loved. Like a language, we have different ways of understanding love. Maybe you feel most loved when someone tells you you're brilliant, but they don't feel loved until they spend two hours of quality time playing a game with you.

One of the biggest mistakes I see people making in modern dating and relationships is assuming that how they feel loved is how their date feels love. It's easy to assume that someone else receives love the same way you receive love. Imagine that you love words of affirmation, so it feels important to chat with someone for a couple of weeks on a dating app before committing to a date, but their love language is physical touch. They may lose interest before you, but not because you aren't fabulous. They simply don't feel that you're interested in them. When you date as a great seductress, your mission is to share how you receive love with your dates and to discover how your date feels the most loved. Which language do you need to feel loved by someone?

To practice receiving, pick one love language to focus on this week. Then, whatever you choose, practice *receiving* it from everyone around you. When you set your intention to receive, really *receive*. Often, really receiving means pausing and putting your feminine presence into the exchange that is going on. Notice the difference in the relationship between you and the other person when you make space for and take in what they offer.

Choose one of the love languages:

1. **If you choose Physical Touch** - look for opportunities to receive hugs, handshakes, pats on the back, and, depending on your lifestyle, embraces and sex.

2. **You choose Words of Affirmation** - this means praise, encouragement, or the words "I love you." When you receive compliments and acknowledgments, allow them to soak in. Rather than denying or minimizing them, express thanks.

3. **You choose Receiving Gifts** - practice receiving gifts you are offered with grace and gratitude. Notice even small offers, like being handed a pen to sign your name or a stranger's smile.

4. **You choose Acts of Service** - this is the one I started with because I had so much resistance to receiving help. My favorite practice was seeing whether strangers would open a door for me. Ten out of ten times, they would - men and women. You must pause slightly before reaching the door. Then, as you walk through,

give them an acknowledgment, "thank you." Use eye contact and a smile if it feels genuine. If you look at them and acknowledge their service, you will probably notice joy creep onto their face from this simple exchange of service and gratitude.

5. **You choose Quality Time** - look for opportunities to engage with people in ways that make you happy. Phone your friend, spend a morning in a coffee shop with someone or have dinner with your family. Be in your feminine presence with them and receive their presence.

And, of course, practice as many of these as you'd like on and with dates. I especially recommend practicing the categories that are uncomfortable or difficult for you. By the end of all your practicing, you may know the ultimate truth: *that receiving is giving.*

TL;DR

1. Receiving is feminine energy, while masculine energy is giving.

2. During seduction, focus on what you receive in dating rather than what you can give.

3. When men feel they have nothing to give you, they will be less attracted to you and unlikely to commit to you.

4. Receiving can feel more challenging for people with deeply internalized self-sufficiency or unworthiness stories.

5. Get in touch with what you want so that you know when to receive and when to say "no thank you."

6. The most charming and irresistible way to receive in dating is graciously.

7. Begin to reframe giving and receiving from a commodity transaction that requires repayment to a relational transaction that creates a connection.

8. Masculine energy people thrive on purpose. Part of building rapport with a masculine person is allowing them space to have purpose in speaking with you, being with you, and perhaps building a life with you. Practice receiving support from your dates, and then practice asking for support.

9. When it comes to you receiving attention and love, practice makes perfect.

CHAPTER 6

SHIFT TO PHYSICAL

Feminine energy is grounded in the physical - it is centered in the body. Masculine energy is mental - it is centered in the head. Shifting from masculine to feminine energy requires one thing. Get. Out. Of. Your. Head.

Your head is sabotaging you as a feminine person dating. All strategizing, scheming, organizing, and then re-organizing your day around dates hinders you in love rather than supporting you. Your body contains your feminine magic, your physical, emotional, and energetic safety. Your body will also reveal your true feelings about your date and your intuition about how well the connection is going. You must practice making relationship decisions from your body rather than calculations and logic from your head. Humans do not behave logically (whatever that means) in relationships, and a meaningful relationship is not based on strategy or playing a game to win love.

Whatever witty thing you think you can say to win him, only say it to express your true self. If you go on a date with someone you're unsure about, don't be surprised when it doesn't lead to deep attraction. Attraction is unlikely to occur if your body is not on board. You may even experience anxiety if you have planned out your entire relationship from the first date to 80 years old, holding hands in rocking chairs. Your brain will try to figure out *how to make it happen*, and you will spend your energy there instead of getting to know the actual man you are dating. Chasing mental fantasies will not support you to be wanted by the man in front of you.

Your brains and logic are part of you; they cannot be separated. Using your mind to fantasize can be useful in life because your daydreams point to your true desires. But when you want to create attraction and connection, using lots of mental energy will not serve you as a great seductress. Thoughtfully re-organizing your calendar so you can see your date when it works best for him will not get your sexual energy moving. Strategizing "how to get the man" or spending excessive energy choosing the best date outfit, location, time, and scenario will not help you become a woman who is lit up inside and irresistible to the men right in front of you, ready to date you. If you catch yourself in the "what to do," "what to say," or "what to think," mental space, return to your body first.

When you connect to your body, you will be able to notice the level of sexual tension being created between you and your date. This is because chemistry takes place in the body. If you don't feel any physical excitement or intrigue for your date, they are probably a bad fit for you. Shifting into awareness of your physical presence is the first step to becoming fabulous at creating the second ingredient of seduction: sexual tension.

Inside Your Body

I used to think about my body from the outside, as in *how I look to you*. The feminine energy approach to your physical body is *how I feel inside*. Feminine energy is about the sensations and experience of living inside your body. Your feminine energy is the experience of being you from the inside.

Have you been practicing deep breathing and getting connected to your own being? I hope you answered yes, because here comes the next step. What do you notice about your physical state? Become aware of sensations in your body. Notice whether you are warm or cold. Are you feeling sensations of anxiety? Is there a knot in your stomach? Are you elated? Breathe into any feelings that put you in your head and then return your attention to your body. Are you hungry or thirsty? In seduction, it doesn't matter what you are perceiving; what matters is the feelings in your body. Practice noticing your body when you search for matches on dating apps, and when you chat with potential dates, speak to dates, go on dates, and become intimate with your date.

Your Energetic Power Center

There is one more tool to use in the feminine energy of being and connecting to your physical experience. It is activating and using your energetic power center. Feminine energy and life force power reside between the hips. You can access your power at any time, in public or private, standing, sitting, or lying down. You are never without your personal power because it is inside you.

Wherever you are now, sitting, standing, or lying down, begin with the breathing awareness practice we learned in Chapter 4. Then, breathe into the space between your hips. Identify a center point between your hips toward the back of your spine, around 2 inches below your belly button. This is the womb space, where a child begins to grow in a female body. All human lives begin in this place.

Focus on that center point. Notice changes in your body. Breathe into that center point. Try it again standing up, sitting down, lying down, and walking. Are you always able to find that breath and center point?

Don't stop here if it is difficult, or you feel confused, or like you don't feel anything. Practice. Just a few times a day, whenever it crosses your mind (or when an attractive person crosses your path), focus on the center point between your hips and breathe all the way down into that space. The womb is the power center for feminine creation and energy, but you do not need to have a womb to access its power. You are accessing an energetic point.

I began practicing this while waiting in line at grocery stores. I stood there surrounded by people, becoming aware of my body. My back tended to straighten up, and my breath became more accessible and less anxiety-ridden. Next, I practiced while walking down the street. Notice how you walk differently when you focus on the point of your power.

Your hips may need time to feel comfortable getting attention, or they may feel freer right away. Let them move naturally. There may or may not be more or less swing. Is your back straighter or more curved? What happens to you when you connect to your body's power?

Now we are talking about physical presence. Start cultivating your physical presence today. It is what will make people notice you are attractive and sexually intriguing. Becoming aware of your physical presence is a process; practice it regularly. Think about your power center when you lie down to sleep and when you brush your teeth in the morning. Concentrate on your power center when you walk into a restaurant or room that makes you a little nervous. Keep your eyes on the path you are walking and your mind centered on the power between your hips.

Consult your power center whenever you need extra support and you're feeling tempted to do something in dating from stress, desperation, or your need to prove something to a man. When you go to reply to a text, make sure you can feel your power center. When something he says makes you uncomfortable, return to your power center before proceeding. When you're sitting across from him and feel so much attraction you're unsure what to say, dive deep into that power center.

Inside your body, you always have the energetic power of your being.

Body Talk

Whether or not you are aware of it, other people react to you based on your body language. Your energy subconsciously affects your posture, gestures, and facial expressions and are usually the first cues other people have about who you are and how to treat you—your energetic body matters.

Begin to notice your physical reactions when interacting with people, and especially your physical sensations around people you are attracted to or from whom you are receiving intense attention.

I used energetic awareness just today when a strange man approached me on the street and aggressively got in my face. I was able to breathe into my nervousness at the unknown situation, and I imagined expanding my energy. Without me even having to speak, the stranger watched my face and then backed down and moved on without another word.

You can practice awareness and expansion of your energetic body in everyday life and dating. First, breathe in and notice yourself, and then notice your physical reaction to the other person or people around you. Is your throat tightening? Are our fists clenched? Is your energy shrinking in on you like an internal shrug? Next, become aware of where your body is in space. How close are you to other people? Is it comfortable for you? Would moving somewhere else be more comfortable for you? Do you wish to be closer to someone, or farther away?

If you feel your body tensing or shrinking, expand into your own physical space by imagining a protective circle or globe of light expanding around you. You do not necessarily need to speak or move, but notice your energetics. Imagine the globe of light is your personal space that no one gets to violate unless you invite them. See the edges of your personal globe and notice the integrity of your energy.

You may notice yourself standing taller and commanding more attention. Connect to the power center between your hips if you ever feel nervous. Remember the life force you are and that you contain. Practice being in your own physical space. You have two choices after noticing your automatic physical reactions. You can simply breathe and allow them, or you can take steps to change your physical environment so you feel turned on and sexy. Most importantly, be in your body and see how it changes the way people treat you.

Rebound Tour Guide

After Austin, I was heartbroken in a new way. I began to feel a sneaking suspicion that something was truly wrong with me. I had been actively dating for six years at that point, and I had never felt truly wanted. I had never had that song-worthy love where our conversations lasted for hours, and we couldn't keep our hands off each other. I wanted that. I wanted a love that lit up my life. I felt like I saw so many people experiencing it and it was never my turn.

I got a job as an Adventure Tour guide, driving foreigners around the US in large vans and dropping them off for nights in the best tourist locations America has to offer. The tour guide culture included a lot of stress, drinking, and casual sex. My training group generated several couples, but I was not one of them. Once again, my belief that I was ignorable, forgettable, and awkward was confirmed.

One night I gave in to the culture, got very drunk on tequila, and allowed a fellow tour guide to push me home in a shopping cart, after which we had awkward, drunken sex in the back of a passenger van. He wanted to keep seeing me (or was it to keep sleeping with me?), but I did not feel attraction, sexual tension, or an emotional connection with him. I also felt a certain level of shame and worry that other people knew. I wasn't particularly proud of myself and wasn't romantically fulfilled.

He was, however, a very kind and generous person who came with me to pick up a GPS I had bought from Craigslist, and I was grateful for his support as I met a stranger in a parking lot to make the exchange. Afterward, we drove to San Francisco together from Santa Rosa to pick up a stranded friend.

I exclaimed, "Look at that sunset; it's so beautiful!"

And he said, "Oh my god, it's so beautiful it reminds me of you."

His tone was slightly sarcastic, and I laughed off the comment with, "Aww, so sweet." Then I was quiet as I tumbled headlong into a hole of mental chatter.

This was only the second time a man had called me beautiful in my life. The first one was a Portuguese cell phone repair man who unlocked my SIM card in Geneva, Switzerland. I fell madly in lust with him immediately after he uttered the words "you're so beautiful" as I handed him my phone. He was tall and imposing, and energy seemed to course through his body even as he stood still and gently removed the old SIM card and replaced it with a new one. Eight weeks later I ran into him at a street festival.

"When I see your lips, I want to kiss you," he said as a greeting.

"What are you waiting for?" I asked, and we made out on the spot. We spent the next afternoon at the beach together, and then I slept with him a week later. He hadn't asked to see me again nor remained in contact. It was my first one-night stand. *I must be at least somewhat attractive to men if they'll call me beautiful and sleep with me. I just want more. Am I worth more? Does being more loved exist? Am I too difficult to love?*

I thought about the man in the car next to me who was over ten years older than I was. *If he is pushing young drunk girls home in shopping carts at this point in his life, will he ever grow up? Is his maturity likely to get better, or will it get worse? When he is 50, I'll be 38, and our health levels will probably be very different. Will I still be doing this job in 10 years? Has this all been a terrible rebound mistake?*

I drove on as the sun set fully, and my mind tried to find solutions to questions I couldn't possibly know right then. Rather than engaging him in a conversation that might have told me more about him, I stayed quiet and let him run the show. He told more jokes and made me laugh long and hard, and then his tour left town three days later. He didn't say anything sexy like he hoped to see me on the road, nor did we remain in contact.

Masculine Mental Chatter

When you're in your mind chatter, you are in masculine energy, so you are creating less attraction, less sexual tension, and less emotional connection by being there. At all points during seduction, focus on your physical experience over the chatter your brain shares with you. When you're messaging a new connection on a dating site, avoid ruminating about what he thinks of you, his intentions, and what you could become to each other.

Whenever you put that energetic attention on him and his desire, you've taken it off yourself and thereby sacrificed your power. You're also less focused on getting to know who your potential partner is because you're so busy predicting your future with him based on your past experience. Take your power back by focusing on your own energy. Feminine energy is inward-moving. Move the energy toward yourself by keeping the focus on your body. You will be incredibly surprised at how well the conversation flows and how intriguing you are to him when you are having a conversation while connected to your body and feminine presence.

Notice whenever you're dancing with mental chatter about any aspect of dating, even before you're in connection with a man. Whenever you're worrying about the cute guy across the room that you body flirted with (see the flirting exercise at the end of this chapter for a How-To) because you don't know whether he got the message, return your attention to your own body.

If your looks are a reason you give yourself for not finding a real relationship, you're probably experiencing masculine mental chatter around your physical appearance. Remember, your appearance is not the deciding factor in true attraction and seduction. For the sake of dating, quiet mental chatter around your body and appearance in favor of going inside your body and asking it how it feels.

Rather than thinking, *ugh, these thighs. No wonder no one wants you.* Or, *these crows' feet are hideous. If I could fix them, dating would be easy.* Turn your focus to the experience of being inside your body. Continuously ask your body how it's doing internally. Beyond anxious or negative mental chatter, you want to quiet the voices in your head as much as possible. Make dating decisions from body awareness.

When my now husband told me he loved me two weeks after meeting, I checked in with my body. My first instinct was to freak out and get in my head about how it was too soon and what other people would think, but instead, I chose to go straight down to the point of my power and check in with *myself* about the idea of him loving me. Inside my body, I was not afraid at all. I felt very warm and comfortable and completely held and cherished by him. I looked into his eyes and felt lit up by his presence. From my physical awareness, I realized that love was an experience beyond mental conception. But that glow of warmth in the connection between him and me was love.

"I love you, too," I responded.

Whenever you find you are up in your head (worried about what others think, worried about proving your worth to a man, concerned about what he is thinking, worried about what you look like, anxious about what to say), return your attention to being in your body and what you *feel* like. Your body knows what you need.

Dating From Your Body

As much as you feel comfortable, allow the masculine partner to figure out the mental parts of the date. Where are you going? What time will you meet? What will you do? Allow the masculine to lean into his mental energy during seduction.

Guide him with your parameters and your desires: *I am free on Saturday. I want to go on a picnic. I love ice skating. I want to be out in nature more. I love the theater and haven't been to a show in ages. I would love to go to the symphony.* Tell a man exactly what makes you happy and see what he does. A man who is ready to love you will use his mental energy to create your desires, but you have to tell him what they are.

Hand him your desire and see what he comes up with from his masculine energy. Allow the masculine partner to worry about what to say to start the conversation and how to "fix" any perceived issues that come up during the seduction phase. Smile at him or give him an invitation with your energy, so he knows you're open for conversation. When a fork drops on the floor at a restaurant during your first few dates, don't immediately bend over to grab it. Fight your urges to "fix" everything and observe his reactions. This will teach you so much more about what kind of man he is than if you do everything you can to keep the connection alive and work to make everything "perfect."

Your body is also important to consider *before* you head out on a fabulous date. How are you feeling that day? Are you low energy? You will likely not have the greatest date if you are dehydrated, sleep-deprived, or on an emotional edge for any reason. Take care of your physical needs beforehand. Respect yourself and your energy first and call to reschedule rather than push through if you aren't doing well. Seductive energy requires you to be lit up from the inside, which is hard to feel when you are sick or emotionally exhausted. Pay attention to your body while you are on a date. Are you cold? Are you comfortable? Are you hungry or thirsty? Are you turned on? You will need this information for the emotional communication practices we will look at in chapter 8.

How does this man's presence make you feel? What kind of attention does he pay to you and your body? Keep in mind that the attention starts with you. When you notice and focus on your body, he will too. Consciously or unconsciously, when you are both more focused on your bodies, there will be greater sexual tension. If you are not outright flirting, you can bet there will be body scanning on his part as you look down your own arm at the glass in your hand. Building sexual tension can be either subtle or unmistakable. When you sink into your body, placing your focus there instead of on your mental process, you will automatically become more sensual.

Trust Your Gut

Notice that your point of feminine power is in your gut. Trust it. When you check in with your belly and feel unease, tightness, or nausea, it means you don't trust someone; don't put yourself at their mercy. Don't get in their car. When something feels off, don't agree to date them. When they offer to extend the date, and you don't want to, say, "No, thank you."

Uneasiness in your senses means it's prime time to practice having your masculine (mental *doing* energy) assert your feminine needs and wants (physical state and desires). Notice what you really want from your feminine intuition and express it from your masculine.

During my tour guide season, I went Salsa dancing and met a man I wasn't physically attracted to, but I said yes when he asked me out for the next weekend. We went to dinner at a fabulous Puerto Rican bar and then met up with his friends to go salsa dancing. He was an interesting and well-behaved man. I felt relatively neutral about his looks but warm about his character.

I still said "okay" when he dropped off his friends at 2 am after dancing and suggested we go to his house. Likely, he understood this consent to mean I was interested in sleeping with him. But I was still reeling from the night, the alcohol, the dancing, the people, and the things I was learning. I simply hadn't taken a moment to check in with my body and said "okay" with no physical awareness. When we reached the silence of his apartment, I realized I just wanted to go back to my hotel and try to sleep. I needed to drive eight hours down the coast of California in four hours.

Letting me leave was not his plan. He cajoled me, sweet-talked me, and made out with me as a way of keeping me there. I did not say no, demand a ride, or walk out the door. He was not mean or aggressive, but I was paralyzed with indecisiveness and unable to communicate effectively. It became clear beyond a doubt that he wasn't interested in driving me home until we had sex. I didn't know where I was nor feel rich enough for a taxi, so I submitted.

I lay there while he did what he needed to, and then I quietly re-dressed myself. He drove me home right away, and I slept two hours before my 6 am drive. He checked in on me later that day, and I responded that *I was fine; the drive had gone well, thank you.* I told him I would get his advice when my tour reached New York City, where he had grown up. What I had discovered was numbing my body. I noticed sex did not physically hurt when I didn't care about the person I was sleeping with.

If you experience numbness in sex or around your feelings of sexuality and love, know that your body is giving you valuable information that you are disconnected from it. Your highest level of relationship does not include habitual disconnection or disassociation from your body. Allow your body to help you date better.

During my "rebound" phase from Austin, I did not know about using my masculine energy to protect myself in ways like speaking up for myself or setting clear boundaries. I usually wasn't connected to my body, desires, and feminine energy enough to even know what I wanted - my desire on that night was to go home. Know what you want so you can ask for it. Ask your body what it needs so you can fulfill those needs or express them to your dates.

Start with how the body feels rather than what the head thinks. When your body doesn't feel good, it's time to go. And vice versa, when you feel fabulous, allow yourself to bask in your date's company, words, and attention. Your body knows a good thing, too.

Your Body As A Temple

Your body is a temple, and it exists just for you. It is your home, and it governs much of what happens in your life, whether you are aware of it or not. The way you treat your body matters. You may have heard the phrase *mind over matter*, which has sometimes been interpreted as the power to use will to control your physical urges. You think if you just had a stronger brain, you wouldn't binge on Oreos and milk late at night. You think that if you could just control your mind you would get more done at work. If you could make your brain force your body into doing its will and what it knows is right, you would have your ideal life.

The higher quality approach I recommend is mind *with* matter - mental *with* physical. You can push yourself mentally, but if the body is not along for the ride, it will get sick, burn out, or lose the ability to feel joy. Your body matters as much as your mind, and it is your partner in life.

Dating will change for you when you begin to honor your body as a partner in life. In dating, sex, and love, much of your personal power lies in the feminine wisdom of your body. Everything we have discussed so far: your appearance, your relationship to being, your capacity to receive, and your physical body are yours to nurture and protect.

When you start to take care of your body, you will find that your body takes care of you. By treating your body with more love, you will begin to love your body more. There are all kinds of doctors, programs, books, and resources out there to help you change your relationship with your body and your physical habits if you desire or require deeper support around your body.

The journey of caring for your body is lifelong, and your needs will vary over time. For me, different stages of taking care of my body have included things like: going dancing more often, going to the doctor when sick instead of toughing it out, getting massages, taking electrolytes, or learning to rest, among other wellness practices.

In energetic terms, it comes down to this question again: Does your masculine energy serve your feminine energy? Do your own actions around feeding, hydrating, washing, resting, nurturing, and noticing your body serve your best health and vitality? Do your own words about your body help you to feel your best? That said, be aware of the trap of perfectionism on your journey with your body. Thinking that you need a perfect body, believing that you are trying to create the ideal body, and believing that you need to think your body is perfect are all traps!

Quick myth-busting: Whether your body is large, small, thin, hourglass, round, or crooked, you are already lovable. The perfect body is a mythical concept - likely unattainable because it is so undefinable. A healthy body is fabulous, but many people live with illness and still create love. You do not need to achieve bodily perfection to create love. You don't need to wait for total physical health and fitness to become powerfully attractive.

Believing you need to love your body and wellness level fully and totally before you find a meaningful relationship can be a trap or an excuse to hold off on dating. Oftentimes as women, our relationship with our bodies is complex and even painful. It can take a long time to heal our bodies and emotions around our shape. The point I want to make is that wellness and body love are journeys, not destinations. There is nowhere specific you have to be in order to attract love. Take things one day at a time and one step at a time. Just remember that the person who will *always* be near your body is you. I invite you to honor your feminine energy and treat your body with as much love and respect as possible. What is one thing you could start doing daily to treat your body with love?

Exercise: the Body Flirt

Flirting is an important part of dating. Creating sexual tension is largely about flirting, and you need sexual tension to create a juicy romance. Otherwise, you may end up in some lackluster, one-heart-in, one-heart-out situationships.

The best way to begin learning the art of flirtation is the Body Flirt. Ease into flirting by practicing the physical aspect of the art. You can flirt without saying a word. Body language is a powerful communicator. You don't even need to be in person. When you position yourself flirtatiously during a phone call, for example, the energy of the call will be different. Your words and conversation will have a more alluring tone. Use Body Flirting during any and all dating activities, from searching dating sites for matches to any in-person meeting.

Practice and use these body techniques:

1. Get in touch with yourself internally. How are you feeling?

2. Feminine energy is non-linear, so position yourself asymmetrically whenever possible during seduction. Asymmetrical means unevenness or no straight lines in your body posture. Here are several asymmetrical body placements to try on for size. When sitting: lean back with your shoulders relaxed. Leaning back creates asymmetry. Cross your legs. When standing: tilt one hip out to the side or keep one shoulder higher than the other. Keep one hand on your hip and place the other somewhere else. If you touch your face, have your hands at different places rather than both cupping your cheeks or touching both ears. Let your body relax and sink luxuriously into whichever position you choose.

3. Place your hands on your body. The collarbone is a seductive place for a finger to land. Touching your hair with one hand and making direct eye contact for a moment before looking away. Keep asymmetry when placing your hands.

4. If you are going to move (or need to fidget), do it slowly. Slow, repetitive movements are sensual rather than distracting or anxiety-producing.

5. Undress slowly and carefully - men love this for obvious reasons - but all you need to do is sensually take off a coat to inspire the image of you taking off other articles of clothing.

6. Be intentional with your eye contact. Remember the power of asymmetry and indirectness - glance over or up at a romantic potential. If you feel extra bold, scan their body and smile.

These techniques are powerful for two reasons, they create more sensuality in your movement *and* your own emotions, and they can be seen and interpreted unconsciously by others as signs that you are sensual and intriguing. In other words, they make you *feel* flirty, which makes you behave more flirtatiously.

Start implementing today!

TL;DR

1. Feminine energy governs your physical space, whereas masculine energy rules your mental space.

2. In addition to practicing your breathing and keeping your central nervous system regulated, practice becoming aware of the energetic space around your physical body.

3. At all points during seduction, focus on your physical experience over the chatter your brain engages in.

4. As much as you feel comfortable, allow the masculine partner to figure out the mental parts of the date.

5. You have immense life force power between your hips. Use it to ground yourself whenever necessary, especially in dating situations.

6. Trust your body and your gut to tell you what you need to know about the connection between you and your dates.

7. Use your masculine energy to act upon or assert what your body determines you want and need.

8. Your body is a temple, and it exists just for you. It is your home, and it governs much of what happens in your life, whether you are aware of it or not. The way you treat your body matters.

9. Use the Body Flirt during any and all dating situations.

CHAPTER 7

SHIFT TO WILD

One of the most powerful shifts you can make in seduction is from masculine structure to the feminine wild. Structure is defined, predictable, and linear, wild energy is chaotic, unpredictable, and unknown. Your power to relate to a new person lies in your ability to be in the wild - the unknown - of who that person is. You must accept that you don't yet know what they want and where the relationship is going. The wild is where you do not know, do not assume, and do not expect perfection.

Wild energy is a place that scares people because the masculine part of our thinking wants to predict all activities around us in order to keep us safe. Unfortunately, your masculine thinks safe means what you have already experienced or felt. A known discomfort is better than any unknown potential for your masculine energy. The unknown is dangerous. And yet, what you want right now is to experience a deeper, more fulfilling, more exciting love than you ever have before. You want to head into the wild unknown.

Fear of the wild can get especially activated in dating because we learn about love and connection in childhood and infancy. We subconsciously expect creating romantic relationships to feel like the attention we received back then when connection meant survival instead of romance. We get into our survival feelings quickly in dating.

We think we know what attraction, connection, and love look and feel like. We assume we know what other people are thinking and feeling about us. We believe we can predict their actions and feelings without asking them directly.

Wild energy is the place where you stop making these assumptions and predictions because you are in the unknown paradigm of a new person. This is where the deep connection between people truly exists. When you do not assume you know who someone is, what they are thinking, and how they feel, you can get to know who they really are.

Your wild feminine energy lets you relate to the chaotic, messy, and imperfect parts of yourself and others in a loving and healthy way. In a feminine chaotic space, two things can be true at the same time. For example, your thoughts and my thoughts are equally true, even when they appear contradictory at first. In an intimate relationship, your needs and my needs are equally important. Multiple realities and truths exist at the same time. Once you can hold the energy of the wild in your body, you will be able to relate to someone in a healthy manner. The highest levels of intimacy are possible for you when you befriend the paradoxes of life.

Chaos also makes room for the both/and principle. You love him, AND he isn't the one for you. The sex and communication are great, AND you still don't want to be with him long-term. You want to be fierce and independent, AND you want a loving and connected relationship. You are imperfect, AND you are hot as hell. Once you can hang with wildness, you will be able to process and allow the both/and reality of your thoughts, emotions, needs, and wants.

You will find that many negative, destructive, and controlling relationship behaviors take up less of your time once you make friends with the wild. You will be much better at being present with people, showing up honestly as yourself, and connecting authentically and deeply. Healing your relationship to the energy of wildness and unpredictability may require deep work with a therapist or coach. I highly recommend taking on that healing. It will profoundly change your life and all your relationships, not just romantic encounters.

Wild Love

I moved to Romania to see the East meet the West for myself. I wanted to learn more about the post-communist world and create a personal relationship with Eastern Europe. East-West relations had been the focus of my Political Science degree at university. My college mentor arranged for me to get a job in Bucharest, which was the only encouragement I needed to pack a bag and cross the ocean.

Romania is a beautiful and wild country. It has yet to recover from the historical events of the past 100 years. History seems to brush up against modernity all over the country. Old buildings are crumbling into dust, right next to grand and sometimes imposing neoclassical, Byzantine, and communist architecture. Extravagant churches decorated with detailed paintings and gold accents stand grandly in the middle of both commercial and residential areas or pop into view unexpectedly when you turn a corner. Everywhere, people drive fast cars and wear the latest fashion from British designers, but they also wear traditional floral headscarves tied at their chins and cart groceries, goods, and documents around on foot. Romania is a land of paradoxes and wildness.

The wind blows hard and fast down narrow streets and wide boulevards in Bucharest. I fell in love at first sight with the crumbling architecture and the overgrown vines crawling over the city's stone walls. I loved walking down the cobblestones of the main center or along the banks of the canal that is the Dambovita river. The sun seemed to shine sharper there than on my native Oregon. I felt more vitality in the air. It felt like the sun and wind could power me through life without me having to push so much. I fell hard and fast for Romania.

I met Cristian during my first week at my new job in Romania. Our boss introduced us to each other twice, and we were both very polite about the second time. Neither of us mentioned that we'd already met. We just shook hands again with grace and a twinkle in our eyes. Cristian's presence was calm and steady. I knew immediately that there was something I appreciated about him. He always had music playing in the background, like a soundtrack to his life, and when he smiled, his whole face crinkled up in happiness.

I was his Romanian Accent Reduction instructor. In our first lesson together, we looked at English vowel sounds, of which there are at least 21, compared to Romanian's seven vowels. We chatted about our favorite music. In the second lesson, we looked at the schwa, a special sound in English that replaces a strong vowel whenever its syllabic importance is reduced. It sounds like "uh," as in "Uh-LA-nuh" instead of "Alana." Cristian and I discussed our homes and basic family life, which is common in second-language learning.

"I have *an* older sister," He said.

"I have *a* younger brother," I said.

Lessons with him were the most relaxing of all my teaching duties. We had a natural rapport and a shared love of music.

I had been in the country for two weeks when I ran into him and his best friend, Andrei on the street. I was on my way home, loaded down with groceries.

"We're going out. Come with us!" they said.

I protested that I was carrying groceries. Internally, I was wondering about the boundaries between my corporate students and me. I had not been given an office or benchmarks to do my job. I had been given exactly one instruction: do not date anyone in the company. But there on the street weighed down with a large pack of toilet paper and heavy glass jars of pre-made food, I did not feel that I was in a position of power. Andrei insisted that I join them with more verbal force than I was used to, coming from my own passive, slightly apologetic US west coast culture. In Romania, people communicate very directly and are unafraid to use higher emotional states, like anger, excitement, and scolding in their speech. I was no match for his certainty and insistence. Andrei took the bags out of my hands and carried them to my apartment himself, saying we would catch up with Cristian.

I knew the secret of language learning, which is that you learn more when you're having fun than when a teacher writes vocabulary on a blackboard. I decided it was an extension of my duty to spend recreational English time with them. I also really wanted friends.

We went to a small pub - their favorite, they told me - and they filled me in on Romanian cultural norms through their eyes. They told me I should stop shaking hands with people because it was a rude gesture for a woman. They taught me about mainstream Romanian music and laughed as I tried to understand and pronounce slang. They also asked me endless questions about my life. I was used to meeting Westerners while traveling, who mostly wanted to know about my home country's culture and political landscape. Westerners ask safe, personally-distant questions. In Romania, people are comfortable asking you about your personal life and emotions. Andrei was brash and confrontational, and Cristian was kind and thoughtful.

I found myself sharing things about my life with these two men that I had never said out loud before. No one had ever asked. It was immediately comfortable and fun, perhaps thanks to the large amount of alcohol I consumed and the larger amount they consumed.

"If anyone gives you any trouble, you find us, and we will take care of it," they told me. I was offered explicit protection by men who were not just willing to listen to my thoughts and feelings but were outright asking for them. I had never been treated this way. I already suspected Cristian was the best man I had ever met.

I drank too much, and Cristian walked me home, leaving me respectfully at the door to my building. I already knew that I wanted him, but I also knew nothing was allowed to happen between us, so I banished thoughts of us being together from my mind. I was highly disciplined when it came to doing as I was told. This did not, however, calm the sexual tension between us.

I took him and Andrei up on their offer of protection, but the only real safety I needed was a calm place to work. I hadn't been assigned a desk or space in an office, and I bounced around departments teaching the Security Team, the lead Generation team, and the Tech team. The Security Manager did not welcome me in their office outside strict class time, and the Lead Generation Manager disliked something about my teaching; perhaps that I was young, female, and his authority figure, so he spent all our sessions bullying me instead of following my directions.

I needed a place to land and collect myself after being in so much emotional space. In Cristian's office with the tech team, I felt safe and valued. All the guys there were kind and considerate, and yes, probably would have slept with me if they had the chance. But we didn't talk about that. We talked about music and life, and I graded assignments and wrote new ones while they typed away on their computers. They would buy me tiny two-ounce coffees from the vending machine, which I received with delight.

Cristian and Andrei took me out again the next week and had me try white rum. The glass was small, so I took it as a shot. They balked, then got me another one. I downed it as a shot again, and they burst out laughing.

"What are you doing?!" They exclaimed.

"Shots!" I replied.

"That's not a shot," they said, pulling themselves together to educate me.

Apparently, this tiny serving of rum was intended to be sipping alcohol. Unsurprisingly, I was drunk at the end of the night, and Cristian walked me home again. This time a gentle late-night rain fell all around. We walked close together as he held the umbrella over us.

"I hate the rain usually, but here it's not so bad," I told him.

Christmas came, and I went away to spend the holidays with some friends in Germany. Christmas Eve, I received a message from Cristian, a simple holiday greeting. My world flooded with warmth. I wrote him back. Our conversation continued smoothly. He asked me about my trip, and we made text jokes. He wrote smiley faces with multiple parentheses for a mouth. :)))))

I was far from family and usual traditions, but in that text exchange, I had everything I wanted. I felt truly cared about and understood by him. In my gut, I felt that he wanted me as much as I wanted him. I was swirling in a pool of love, joy, and restrained flirtation. I had never experienced someone asking so many questions about who I was. I had never felt that someone was so interested in me, and likewise, I had never felt so interested.

I called my Romanian teacher from university, who had gotten me the job in Bucharest to wish him a Merry Christmas. As we were hanging up, he said, "you be careful with Romanian boys. They are much more charming than Americans."

"I will," I promised him, leaving out the fact that I was already totally lost to love.

I began to go out often with the tech guys, always in groups after someone's shift. Cristian became my number one confidante, explaining Romanian culture to me and listening to my life stories in a way no other man had thought to ask. He would walk me home without fail every time we went out.

By then, it was the dead of winter with snow all around. One night on the walk home, I said I was cold, and then, even though two other guys were walking with us, Cristian took my hand and placed it in his pocket with his hand on top. We continued walking, but my inside world froze.

Were we holding hands? We were kind of holding hands. This seemed like a danger zone in terms of the company rule that I didn't date my students. Hand-holding was undoubtedly romantic.

The excitement rose in my body. I couldn't help myself. I turned my palm to meet his inside his pocket and placed my fingers around his hand. I gently squeezed to let him know what I was feeling for him. He squeezed back. All too soon, the walk home was over, and he once again politely left me at my door. I raced up to my apartment and got ready for bed. But I couldn't sleep. A short while later, he texted me. We wrote back and forth until 4 in the morning—no confessions of love, just fun and playful back and forth. The sexual tension was off the charts.

Being in love with him was utter chaos. Being near him was all I wanted to do. If he was there, no matter who else was around, he was the most important person in the room. When he wasn't there, I thought about him constantly. This was not just attraction; this was an obsession. We hadn't touched beyond our pocket hand-holding. I had moved slowly, smoothly, and unabashedly into love. It was effortless and forbidden.

But we played it cool and professional. And the more we resisted it, the more tension built.

One day, the company's legal support called me into the office. They had been unable to get me a visa and needed one more document - an official paper stating I had no criminal record - before my current visa ran out. I did not want to leave Romania and Cristian, so I spent a day trekking around the city in the frigid air, bouncing between the subway, government agencies, and taxis. It was incredibly stressful as no one seemed to know exactly what I needed and sent me on a few wild goose chases. I needed fingerprints from the Romanian police and documentation from the American embassy. Later, in the safety of the tech office, Cristian scolded me for not asking for help navigating Romanian agencies.

"You have a problem with not asking for help. You don't even speak the language here," he said.

That all-American self-sufficiency was biting me. The whole process might have been a lot easier if I had asked for help from locals or perhaps the company lawyer. Instead, I loaded the whole situation on my own shoulders and suffered the emotional weight of having no visa. Anxiety grew in me. I began checking the mail every day, hoping for the documents to be timely.

But two weeks later, the mail was still conspicuously empty.

One day after work, Cristian and Andrei invited me out for dinner, and I accepted. At the restaurant, I started feeling unwell and not at all hungry, so I didn't order anything. "Eat!" they said when their food arrived at the table. To oblige Cristan, I ate one slice of pizza and immediately felt a little better.

But the next day, my throat had swollen up, and I was congested and hoarse. The day after, I couldn't speak. The cleaning lady came to the apartment, and I collapsed when I stood up to answer the door. I was not sure what was happening to me. Word got out and one of my coworkers insisted on taking me to the doctor. I was diagnosed with a throat infection and given antibiotics. I spent several days slightly delirious on my couch.

When I ventured back out to the world, the visa game was pretty much up. My non-existent police record had not arrived, so when the company's founder visited later that week, it was decided I would return to America to get the document in person.

Sadness engulfed me. My short-lived magical life was either over or on hold for an indefinite length of time. I had no life in my hometown, no home to go back to, and no job, and moving back in with my parents hadn't been part of my life plan. I really didn't like asking for help, especially not from my parents.

Cristian and Andrei invited me out again, and I accepted although I was still weak from illness. The mood was more somber than usual. We talked about my departure.

"I'll be back very soon," I said, trying hard to convince myself.

Andrei, it turned out, had begun a romance with a mystery woman and very suddenly excused himself from our party. Cristian and I were alone at a bar for the first time in our acquaintanceship.

"Do you want to go play pool up the street?" He asked.

"Yes," I said, hoping the night would never end.

We moved on to a bar that was part bowling alley, part arcade, and part pool hall. He ordered more drinks and got the pool equipment. We set up at our table, flirting gently. He let me teach him the American rules to pool, and I let him stand close behind me while I made my shots. The slow, intoxicating tension we had built up over the months was coming to a head.

After a game in which I did quite well, but he snuck in and won at the last minute, he grabbed another drink, and we sat down at a table. He was not usually a man of many words, but he began to monologue. First, he told me how incredible I was and how much he respected my way of being in the world, and then he moved quite suddenly into talking about what he wanted in life - from work, love, and family. He spoke for what felt emotionally like an hour while my heart beat out of my chest. The crack of people striking down bowling pins accentuated the words he spoke. All the secret dreams I had shared with him seemed to match his vision of life.

Could it be that I had finally found someone I wanted who wanted to be with me?

"I want to have a marriage," he said suddenly, "and I think you would be a good candidate for that." He stopped talking and looked deep into my eyes.

My mind went wild.

Masculine Structure

Masculine energy is structured and direct; when a masculine person is ready for love, they create structure around it. By structure in a relationship, I mean commitment, exclusivity, and marriage. These are masculine energy areas.

As a feminine person dating, you likely crave masculine structure, which looks like boundaries, clarity, commitment, and perhaps even marriage. It is not at all wrong or unsexy of you to crave this as a core feminine being. Strong relationships require masculine structure and sometimes, these labels are part of your personal relationship vision. However, during the seduction phase of a relationship, shift your focus from trying to create commitment and certainty. Focus instead on what the connection is like. Find out who your date is so you know if you really *want* their commitment. Spend your energy discerning whether your date is compatible with your vision rather than trying to get him to commit to you. Leave the relationship structure and definition to the masculine partner.

You will be amazed at how quickly a man will ask for commitment with you when you have no pressurized designs on commitment with him. If a masculine person is not asking you for commitment and you want a committed relationship, choose yourself and your vision before him. You will be more attractive and seductive to him if you move on or keep dating other people.

Do not stop dating and creating love with others until you find someone who wants what you want out of a relationship. It is never your job to convince someone to want a certain kind of commitment. It is never your job to fix someone. It is never your job to prove to someone that they would be happier if they just gave you what you want. You will create a lot of un-seductive energy in the connection and stagnant energy in your life if you wait on a man who tells you outright he doesn't want commitment. Date other people.

Do not make ultimatums about commitment with masculine people (ultimatums are also structures); simply continue dating others until you find someone amazing who wants the same future as you. A man who cares about you may agree when presented with a commitment ultimatum, but he will resent it and likely you in the long term. Instead of forcing a man's hand, make your desires clear and direct without communicating that he needs to be the one to fulfill your dreams.

Though it can feel difficult or painful, don't take it personally when a masculine person is not ready to commit to you. You will know they are not ready because they won't ask you for commitment, and they won't take action to prove that they mean business in dating. This is not about you. A man's relationship to commitment is his own, it was formed long before he met you, and it is not a reflection of how much he likes you. He may still be in love with his ex or have some other unresolved issue he is protecting you from by not choosing a structured relationship with you.

If you want to encourage a man who has told you he isn't interested in what you want to change his mind, let him go. Letting him go is the most straightforward way to create clarity for both of you. If your emotional connection is strong, he will come back to you when he is ready. When a man is ready, he will be direct and structured. His energy will be clear and backed up by action. You will have no doubts. If he really doesn't want what you want, he isn't a good man for you. In that case, it's better for you to be out living your life and maybe dating other men instead of pining for him or indulging in your attachment to a fantasy future with him.

That may sound harsh and extreme, but I assure you it can be quite gentle if you are in your relaxed, clear, wild feminine energy. From the beginning, expect the unexpected. Allow yourself to not know who someone is for quite a while. Assume less about their character. Observe who they are before passing judgment on them. How do they handle themselves? Do they follow through with action on the words they speak? Allow yourself the privilege of not knowing where the relationship is going from the first moment you connect. Spend less energy on creating structure and more energy on expressing the full spectrum of who you are, including your wildness, imperfections, and the parts of yourself that you sometimes hide. Is it safe to share these parts with him? Focus on finding out whether he is someone you like and want rather than if and when he will commit to you. You will find that the less concerned you are about convincing a man to commit to you, the faster his motivation to create a relationship structure with you comes forward.

Chaotic Breakdown

I stared at Cristian sitting there in the dim light of the pool hall while flashing colored lights from the bowling alley splashed across his face. He had just told me I would be a good candidate for marriage. Thoughts were exploding through my head all at once.

Candidate is a weird word to use about marriage in English. Would the sentiment have been better expressed in Romanian? Was this sentence unromantic, or was it extra romantic because he was so serious about me? His face was so earnest. *How much had he had to drink? Is this just a drunken moment? How do you respond to something like that? Is this an actual offer of marriage in Romanian culture? We haven't even said we like each other out loud. What will people at work think? Do we have what it takes to be married? What about our cultural differences? Am I willing to spend the rest of my life in Romania?*

Looking back, these questions seem crazy, but at the time, they were actual thoughts passing through my head in rapid succession. I was deep in mental chatter and I had projected far into an unknown future.

"Oh, Cristian," I said slowly, "that's so nice."

Was this the most fear-ridden and pathetic answer I could have possibly given? Probably yes. But at that moment, I was entirely afraid. I was afraid of what "yes, I would like that" would mean for my future. And I was especially terrified of the words, "I'm totally, completely, and hopelessly in love with you," even though they were the honest-to-god truth. If I had had the courage to say those words, my life would have likely taken many different turns than it did. But at the time, because of my projection into the future, it was too much, too big, and too fast. I had no connection to my body. I panicked.

On the outside, we recovered smoothly by going back into our usual safe back-and-forth banter, pretending nothing important had happened between us. Neither of us made grand confessions of love. We simply enjoyed each other's conversation and then left the pool hall. He walked me home as usual but stopped on the street outside my building complex, just out of sight of the security guards.

"Will you call me?" I asked him, turning to face him.

"Every week," he said. "I can call America for free on my phone plan."

We did not kiss goodnight. Was it because I still had a cold? We said goodbye and then turned and walked away, me toward the security guards at my apartment building and him off into the night.

I left the next day, and he did not show up at the bus station to say goodbye to me. I was disappointed, but I comforted myself by saying *when I come back, we'll see how he feels then.* This became my excuse for everything related to him. When I come back, then I'll know what he wants. I did not think much about what *I* wanted.

I arrived back in America and was offered a nannying job, which I accepted despite swearing off nannying completely after my au pair year. *It's only for a month,* I told myself. I ordered the police record my second day back in the US and mailed it express and insured to Romania. It arrived there ten days later. The month passed, and I checked in with the company. They had received my paper, but there was no official word on my visa or my return. I didn't press it further.

Cristian called every week as promised and texted me once in a while. I lived for his voice and words.

What are you up to? I wrote to him.

Work work work work work just like Rihanna, he wrote back.

I laughed silently to myself, but my smile was shrinking. I was working as much as possible by then. I took every babysitting job I was offered and started working at a restaurant. I knew that if America was good for anything, it was making money. So I worked, and I saved. I wanted to have enough money to do whatever came next, and I wished, like anything, it was returning to Romania and marrying Cristian.

The weeks passed and the company was silent. I told Cristian, and he seemed disappointed, but I felt he was disappointed in me rather than in the situation or the company's actions. I would have to stay in America for 90 days for my travel visa to reset. I did not feel joy often except when dreaming of escaping my current reality and choosing the future. I tried to make the most of being back in my hometown, but I felt life draining out of me, the way it does when you aren't doing what you want in life.

My birthday came. I got up at 5 am to babysit. *This is adulthood now,* I thought, *birthdays with 12 hours of work.* In the early morning hours, I sat outside on a blanket in the grass and held the baby. A sweet, dark-haired baby, just like I imagined I'd have with Cristian. He slept peacefully in my arms. Cristian's birthday greeting text came in. I was a bit surprised it wasn't a phone call, but I was happy to see his words anyway. *Maybe he's busy,* I thought. I used a lot of assumption energy to make excuses for people's behavior at the time.

Thank you so much! I wrote back.

I bet you're happy you aren't in Romania with us, he wrote.

What? I replied *it's my biggest regret.*

Where was this coming from? He was upset with me. I was sure of it. I fawned and told him all about how much I wished I was there celebrating the Romanian way. He did not seem impressed nor say all the kind and loving things I wished he would say. I didn't express my sadness or confusion at his words. I bottled it up inside me, interpreting his texts as anger toward me. I assumed he didn't love me anymore. I sat in the grass holding the baby and cried.

For the first time in the two months since we had last seen each other, I doubted that I would return to Cristian and things would play out as I imagined. Him sweeping me into his arms, and me choosing to stay with him, changing the course of my life and my children's lives forever. To confirm my suspicions, he never called again. My grief was complete, and I did not reach out to him. I told myself the usual story. If he didn't want me, then I didn't need him.

But emotionally, I was a mess, and when things got messy, I withdrew rather than face the mess. I could not handle the unknown. I assumed I knew what he felt, what he meant, and what he wanted. Rather than asking him any of these things directly, I stayed in the known by assuming what he thought and felt. At the time, it seemed emotionally safer to do that.

I only had to make it one more month. Then I would be done with the childcare obligations I had agreed to, and I was free to go back to Romania on a new tourist visa. Free to go back to Cristian and find out what our future held. I had a small shrivel of hope, despite the grim assumptions I had made about his feelings for me.

To be a great seductress, you need to be able to hang with the tension of uncertainty. You must be willing to be curious about uncertainty, instead of making assumptions. When things seem imperfect or messy, you must be able to stay connected to your being and your body, without projecting the future and deciding how your romantic connections feel or what they are thinking. If you struggle to feel safe with uncertainty, begin working regularly with the exercises at the end of this chapter.

Messy

Relationships are messy because humans are messy. Your mind is messy, and your emotions are messy. Your inner world holds many paradoxes, contradictions, and nuances. When I say that the feminine is wild, I mean that the feminine is chaotic. It is un-contained, untamed, and unlimited. Feminine energy gets messy. There are places in your life you are afraid to go, and messiness is likely one of them. Many people even associate pain with the messy parts of their life. Can't it be easy? We ask. Can't love be simple? Non-chaotic? It can, but it will never be less messy than you, so you have to get cozy with your uncomfortable messiness first.

Humans who deny chaos are missing half their power. Feminine people who deny their chaos are denying a central part of their power and usually also judging themselves for it. Imagine a world in which I had been able to hold the mess of Cristian's initial confession of interest. Rather than panicking, bottling up my emotions, and replying with something dry, safe, and controlled, I might have actually opened up and allowed him to see the mess of my forbidden attraction to him. The tension inside me might have actually had a chance to express itself and ease up.

Now imagine a world in which I didn't make the assumption that he didn't love me because of our poor communication on my birthday. Imagine I had been friends with the unknown, and I had been able to handle him falling short of the expectation I had, but never voiced directly to him. What if I had noticed what I wanted, and then told Cristian directly that I wanted him to call and shower me with birthday love? Imagine I had told him how much I appreciated and looked forward to his calls. What if he knew that contact with him was my favorite part of my day back then? We often forget that other people don't love the way we love, don't think the way we think, and don't act the way we act. We also forget that they can't read our minds and give us what we expect, want, and need without being told.

Here again, I cannot say what *would* have happened in my past, but in seduction, you will do yourself no favors if you assume what is going on for someone and either withdraw from them or cling to them. Now, you may also have several memories in which you missed the boat on telling someone what you wanted, how they could love you better, and what you expect in love and life. You may be holding onto self-judgment about the things you have done or not done, the things you have been or not been, and the things you have said or not said on your path to true love.

It took me several years to work through the emotions and habits that affected me and my actions during the time I knew Cristian. The mistakes I made were monumental and life-changing. At the time, my responses seemed like the obvious relational thing to do or say. I was uncomfortable with not knowing, so I filled in the gaps in my knowledge with assumptions. I was uncomfortable with uncertainty, so I did my best to control situations and feelings. And I was uncomfortable with anything to do with love that was imperfect. So I opted to reject love.

How To Flirt

So far in this chapter, my story has demonstrated a lot of unhealthy and disempowered ways to create sexual tension. Cristian and I were often hot and messy but rarely on purpose or on the same page. This is largely because I didn't know how to flirt. Flirting is the best way to create empowered sexual tension, but most of us are never explicitly taught what flirtation is and how to use it properly. I changed that for myself and want to change it for you.

At the most basic level, flirting is this:

1. Telling someone you like and/or appreciate who they are or showing that you believe they are worth your time and energy
2. Not expecting a specific outcome from your flirt

This definition of flirting requires that you get connected to your wild feminine energy because it is all about acknowledging what you see in someone else and then not assuming you will receive something in return.

A flirt says, "You're funny. I like you."

There are and will be so many times throughout my story with Cristian where you're probably thinking, *for goodness sake, why doesn't she just tell him she likes him?* I didn't tell him because I didn't know what flirting was and how to do it. I took the act of telling someone I liked them very seriously. It felt heavy and awkward. I felt that chemistry and sexual tension either happened or didn't. Whatever followed in love was a matter of luck. Actually, you can let people know you like them and what you want from them in playful, light, and friendly ways.

Of course, a flirt can also be more assertive and directly sensual or sexual, as in, "Wow, I cannot wait to feel your big hands all over me." As with every element of seduction, there is a spectrum for flirtation, and I recommend you use words that feel natural to you. You can always add new layers of sexy and sexual tension later. Remember that a good flirt is playful and doesn't require your flirtation partner to respond a certain way.

Great flirtation topics are compliments or talking about something fresh, like a fact you just learned, something you just noticed, or something you're passionate about right now. Also, remember that people feel extra interested in people who are interested in them. Ask playful questions.

Begin every seduction conversation with a flirt. Acknowledge something positive about the person speaking to you. On a dating app, compliment their looks, activities, or something interesting on their profile. In real life, make a fun observation about the room, the event, or something you noticed your love interest doing earlier. It's not something serious; you're just saying, "Look at us, here together in this room," or letting the person know they caught your eye in some way. You see them, and they matter. You will have much more compelling, energetically-charged dating conversations if you begin by letting the person know you think they're interesting.

There are also reasons to flirt beyond the purpose of seduction. Flirting builds your mojo and puts you in a spirited state of mind. In that juicy mood, your self-worth and feelings of connection to the world tend to shine a little brighter. Practicing flirtation will hone your skill and confidence with the art of flirting, even if you aren't on a date or specifically hungry for romantic connection. I personally enjoy flirting with my husband every day now. Flirtation is powerful at the beginning of a romantic connection to build sexual tension, but it's also a wonderful, playful, sexy tool to use in other stages of love. You will not regret any effort you put into learning to flirt.

If you need in-depth instruction on flirtation, I recommend the book *101 Ways To Flirt* by Susan Rabin. It will give you more ideas and open your mind to novel flirtatious possibilities.

The Trap of Perfection

The idea of making friends with the wild unknown can be confronting, so I want to add a non-perfection disclaimer here. Wherever you are energetically right now, you are right where you need to be. You are not a hopeless case or behind the curve in your seduction skills. Sometimes we outright avoid our sexual power, flirtation, and the search for love because we decide we aren't finished products yet. We feel we need more healing, more skills, and more perfecting before we are worth the relationship we want. *I need to be perfect to be lovable* is a common subconscious thought for women. *I need to have a perfect body, perfect face, perfect hair, perfect personality, perfect grace, perfect femininity, and perfect accomplishment. I need to say the perfect words at the perfect time. Then I will be lovable and loved. Once I am perfect, then I will be loved.*

The antidote to putting conditions on your lovability is your wildness. Wildness is your feminine birthright. Females birth new lives wildly, not by gently removing the cloth off a stork's basket, but through immense physical effort accompanied by pain, blood, and sometimes screaming. Chaos. Mess. Perfect imperfection. How do you relate to the imperfections you perceive in yourself and the way that you date? Remember to breathe deeply here. How do you perceive your imperfections?

You don't need to have the perfect body. You don't need the perfect face or wardrobe. You do not need to say the wittiest, most romantic, perfect words to catch your match's attention. You don't need to be perfect at flirting, perfect at emotional intimacy, or perfect at dating to find love. *You don't have to be perfect at practicing feminine energy.* Perfection is non-existent, and if you pursue it, you will often find it is a moving target. Both perfection and imperfection live in the feminine energy of chaos. They are impossible to pin down. Work on your expectations of perfection from yourself, your dates, and your relationships through the exercises below. Reach out to a therapist or coach if you need deeper support.

Exercise: Practice Wildness

Choose one or two ways to practice the feminine energy of wildness in your everyday life. If chaos, the unknown, or unpredictability in relationships feel threatening to you, go very, very slowly. There is no one right pace or one right way to work on healing your wild energy. Here are a few suggestions:

1. Practice your everyday awareness of wildness. Observe human interactions, especially situations where there is conflict. Pull your awareness back and look at the broader picture. Observe the "mess" you are perceiving in all its individual parts and in its wholeness. Example: Imagine someone says, "This dress is purple," while someone else says, "This dress is white." Allow your brain to contemplate how this phenomenon can exist. Can two people with "opposite" opinions both be right?

2. Try something new that your brain considers *wild*, and observe how you feel afterward. For example, sign up for a pole dancing class, try a new restaurant instead of the one you always go to on Friday nights, or practice a Body Flirt exercise from Chapter 6 of this book that your brain dismissed as outrageous. Take one, two, or three steps outside your current comfort zone.

3. Meditate "openly," meaning be with yourself without trying to do anything, think anything or nothing, or change anything. Don't even try to relax; simply pause and observe whatever *is*, whatever you think, whatever you imagine, and whatever arises. Allow whatever comes up for you to come up and exist in your brain and body.

4. Make a list of the "mysteries" in your life. Why did he break up with you? Why didn't she write back to you? What would have happened if you had stayed that night? Look at your list and observe what your mind wants to do with these unknowns. What emotions arise for you when you think about what you don't know?

5. Make a list of all the times you believe you behaved "imperfectly" in romantic interactions, dating, and relationships. What are your emotions and thoughts about your lack of perfection? What do you believe is impossible for you because of what happened in your past? What do you believe about other people who are as imperfect as you?

6. *The I-Don't-Know* - Next time a friend, family member, or date tells you the story of a drama in their life, in your mind (not out loud!!), adopt the attitude of *I-Don't-Know*. Every statement they make, respond in your mind with a question. *Is that what really happened? Is that what she said? Is that what it means?* Notice any tendency you have to hear secondhand stories as absolute truth.

TL;DR

1. Feminine energy is the wildness opposite the masculine energy of structure, linearity, and directness.

2. A healthy relationship with wildness, also known as chaos, mystery, unpredictability, and the both/and, is necessary for healthy relationships but may require healing with a therapist or coach to access, understand, or enjoy.

3. Contrary to popular belief, your wildness makes you sexier and more attractive than trying to say, do, and be the perfect thing all the time.

4. I recommend allowing the masculine energy person in the relationship to be concerned about the structure of the relationship (this mostly means labels: exclusivity, commitment, marriage).

5. If a masculine person is unclear about what they want with you, they are usually unclear about what they want in life. If being with someone who is unclear about what they want from

you makes you uncomfortable or unhappy, don't spend your energy there.

6. Interestingly, you will usually find that when you are less concerned about convincing a person to commit to you, their motivation to commit to you increases dramatically.

7. The easiest way to create sexual tension is to flirt. Flirting is a skill that can be practiced and improved.

8. Your messiness and perceived physical, mental, and emotional imperfections are lovable, and because of both/and human relationships, they do not disqualify you from being hot as hell.

CHAPTER 8

SHIFT TO EMOTION

You've probably heard that the way to a man's heart is through his stomach.

Let's bust that myth.

The way to a man's heart is through his heart, and by that, I mean his emotions. You've gotten his attention with attraction, piqued his interest with sexual tension, and you need emotional intimacy to create a sustainable relationship.

And luckily for you, emotion is the energetic realm of the feminine, polarized by the masculine energy of logic. You are primed to create the emotional environment of the relationship. Emotional connection distinguishes you from any other woman your date chats, spends time with, or considers for commitment.

Although men stereotypically do not communicate emotionally with male friends, they are longing to be drawn into the experience of emotional intimacy. All people crave emotional connection with others, men included. Even people who say they say they only care about sex or that they just want something casual are longing for healthy emotional connection. Dating is a great place to practice emotional connection because it will determine the success of your short-term and long-term relationships.

As a great seductress, your power lies in emotion rather than the logic or logistics of dating, meaning where you meet, how often, what activities you do, how to arrive, how to leave, etc. There is no logical solution to connection. Figuring out date logistics is not what creates relationships; emotion is. Emotion is what drives our decisions and actions and determines how much desire someone feels for us. Your ability to connect emotionally is what distinguishes you from anyone else your date is seeing or has dated in the past. The emotional connection between you and him is a singular event, only possible between you two.

No matter what your current emotional intimacy comfort level is, you have the power to create closeness, and this chapter will teach you exactly how. If the idea of creating intimacy is already making you anxious, do not fear, there are ways to create soft connections that don't require bearing your soul. I began as an intimacy amateur, and you can, too. Using the tools in this chapter, I became an intriguing emotional communicator and now have the ability to create emotional intimacy whenever I desire.

The difference between a dating connection that lasts and grows into a full-fledged relationship is a great emotional connection that fulfills both people. Having a great emotional connection is not just luck; it is a skill, and you can learn it and master it starting today. In dating, remember that the power lies in the emotion of the connection, not in the logistics of how dates take place. So keep your focus on the emotion of the connection rather than the rationality or logistics of the match.

Straws That Break

Cristian texted me during my 8-hour layover in Calgary. We flirted in our usual way with songs and random communication. The game was back on. Right after I landed from my 24-hour trip, I planned to meet him and Andrei at one of our favorite pubs.

I landed, dropped my luggage at my new company apartment, changed my shirt, and literally ran the mile to meet him at the pub. My heart was already beating so fast, what did a little extra adrenaline matter? I slowed down once the pub came into view, trying to catch my breath before he saw me. I walked up to them. Cristian was calm and collected. He and Andrei both hugged me. No extra attention from Cristian. Andrei led the interaction. There I was, pretending everything was normal, like nothing had changed and no time had passed, and Cristian and I weren't madly in love. I tried to sneak him secret smiles. No reaction. We moved to a different bar. It was the same kind of night out we used to have as a trio before Cristian told me he wanted to marry me.

Then something new happened. Cristian looked at me with a stern and furrowed brow and told me that I was too nice and that no one could take me seriously. Andrei looked at him surprised, guffawing.

"Damnnn," he said laughing, in a way he had learned from American TV.

Usually, Andrei was the harsh one, and Cristian was excessively kind. I had told many of my friends that he was the kindest man I'd ever met. My heart began aching, and I became less animated, quietly sipping my drink. Being nice was something I liked about myself. Seeing the positive side of people and events was a habit I had purposefully cultivated since childhood. Now the man I loved told me it was a character flaw. I let his words hurt me. Then, I let Andrei carry the spirit of a fun night out for us, and I stopped joining in the laughter. Andrei made a joke that he was going to have to marry me to keep me in the country. I looked at Cristian for a response, but he looked right back at me expectantly.

Was it normal in Romania to make this kind of joke about a woman your friend loved, or had Cristian not told Andrei that he wanted to marry me? The best friend that he called his brother, the brother he claimed knew everything about him. So either Cristian didn't love me anymore, or he hadn't bothered to tell his best friend how much he liked me. I made this observation in a fraction of a second.

"Yeah, right," I said, laughing halfheartedly at Andrei's joke, and then I put my glass to my lips and downed my drink entirely, numbing whatever pain I could while my heart smashed into a thousand pieces.

Push Pull

The way we fall in love includes emotional push-pull, meaning some emotional tension is necessary to create attraction and connection. We feel the joy of seeing someone, the pain of parting, the excitement of reading someone's words, and the fear that we might not see them again after meeting. To create a stable, healthy love, and to stay in love, means having a connection that can hold the emotions of excitement, grief, pain, fun, trauma, equal power, love, and lust, without dipping too far to one side. You don't want to be feeling extremes. Too much stress or excitement, too much lust, and any feeling that you can't live without someone you just met make it difficult to create a real connection with them.

Cristian texted me, ignored me, called me, and didn't tell his best friend he was in love with me. Or maybe he wasn't in love with me. We never exchanged proclamations of love. I had been on many emotional levels with this man, sharing my life stories, fears, and secret dreams that I usually didn't speak out loud. Our relationship was emotionally raw, but we only danced around the edge of our intimate attraction. I had shared so much of myself with him. He shared some details of his life, but not enough to create a deep connection between us. Even on the night he told me he wanted to marry me, neither of us said, "I want you." Much as I had done with Martin in Germany, I was deeply attached to Cristian without having a healthy emotional connection.

You can do better than I did. You can create a healthy push-pull with space for emotions, honesty, openness, and trust. You can create a powerful emotional bond without playing games or sacrificing your emotional well-being. You can get to know someone without attaching out of fear or desperation.

Here's how.

Emotional Questions

In order to create a passionate and intimate emotional connection, use emotional questions from the first moment you speak with a love interest or dating app match. An emotional question is an open-ended question that has a feeling word in it. A feeling word is any verb, noun, or adverb that conjures an emotion, like *want, love, hate, feel,* and also *favorite, worst,* and *best.* Create emotional conversations by asking emotional questions.

Rather than asking a logistical question like, "What do you do?"

Ask, "What do you *love* about your work?" Or "How do you *feel* about your job?" Rather than saying, "Where are you from?" Ask, "Where's your *favorite* place on earth?"

When people answer this kind of open-ended question, they tell you more information about themselves, and they experience an emotional reaction in their own bodies as they talk about something they feel strongly about. Their answer may include what they do for work or a loving reference to their tiny hometown, but they will inevitably communicate something deeper. You'll hear how they think and how they interpret their relationship to work and home. You will have a much more interesting conversation, you will learn more about who they are as a person and what they value, and you will be creating intimacy at the same time.

Facts only go so far. Conversations with emotional questions will allow you to go deeper into intimacy, even from first contact. Notice that the question *What do you love about your work?* is vulnerable but still appropriate to ask someone you've just met. You don't need to pry into someone's past or trauma to create intimacy and trust. You simply have to touch them at an emotional level. Emotional questions go straight to this level by requiring an emotional response. You want them to feel something when they are in conversation with you. Even when you are in the initial chat phase on a dating site, if you are using emotional conversation, they will sense there's something different about talking to you. They will feel seen, heard, and important. They will sense that their thoughts matter to you.

You are looking for someone who can match you emotionally. When they share something funny, hopefully, it makes you genuinely laugh. When they share that they hate their job and want to quit every day, project how this might work for your own lifestyle and beliefs. Does their answer reveal a value that matches your own, or does their answer trigger you? Emotional connection is a top priority in a relationship, and asking emotional questions from the very beginning will give you the best insight into how the other person handles their emotions.

During seduction, communicate as much as possible this way. Not everything you say needs to be an emotional question, but rephrase your questions to be open-ended and contain emotional words as often as you can.

Your communication will change. The quality of conversations that you have with matches and dates will change. The quality of connection you have with dates will differ across the board. It will be obvious much sooner when someone isn't a good match for you. Men will hear you differently and respond to you differently.

When you build a dating relationship with this foundation, you start off with the foundational understanding *I care about what you feel.* This changes everything and sets you up for more success as the relationship progresses. Being emotionally honest is not for wimps, but keep in mind you don't have to rush into sharing your pain and trauma to build trust and rapport with someone. In fact, to create a lasting bond, it's usually better to build up initial trust using softer emotional questions and dive into past hurt around exes, childhood, and grief after you feel secure about your connection. Feeling secure in a connection means feeling safe enough to say what you are thinking and feeling. It means you know you can call or text whenever you want.

Focus on building an emotional connection with your dates, online matches, and interesting men you meet at events or grocery stores. You will begin to see a whole new side of masculine people, and you will start to experience a new paradigm in dating. Communicate in emotion, and you'll be amazed how many men will enjoy speaking to you, spending time with you, and creating a meaningful relationship with you.

Passionate Stalemate

Before I knew how to communicate with men, I was back in Romania, nursing the worst heartache of my life. I was miserable whenever my apartment door closed, and I was left alone with the void of love I perceived. Though I had never been a big tears kind of person, I was constantly sobbing in private, crying myself to sleep most nights, or lying awake staring at the dark ceiling until 4 in the morning. I was secretly an absolute wreck. But it was summer, and there was social fun to be had.

Christian and I continued our facade of friendship. He was still the person I was closest to in the country. Now, however, he had a habit of publicly humiliating me. He would make a jab at my character when we went out with the other guys, sometimes making them laugh but sometimes making us all sit there awkwardly. My heart was broken, and he was breaking it down some more. I realized he was in pain, and it was likely his pain insulting me, but I was frozen by self-doubt as to how to handle the situation. I couldn't spend my life with a man who verbally abused me in public, but I wanted him so badly. What could I say to him to get him to stop treating me poorly?

A woman at the company where we worked invited me to her wedding, which was a week away. It was at a hotel out of town. As a last-minute addition, I was assigned a room with Cristian and Andrei. It was no secret we were close. I traveled with them to the little town and followed them around as they showed me the hotel and wedding venue, explaining Romanian nuptial traditions. A bride has to play the life of the party all night and then cook a huge meal for her old and new family in the morning. They told me we would skip the church part of the wedding because it was boring. Instead, we went to a pub at 4 pm and played drinking games. We ate some food but not much because we were waiting for the enormous wedding feast that would follow. I became drunk quite fast.

We returned to the hotel for the reception at 5 pm, but it turned out that was just so we could get ready. The party didn't start until 8 pm. I had not fully understood what I was getting myself into. A Romanian wedding is an extravagant event that lasts all night and into the morning. The reception hall was decorated with flowers, party lights, and beautiful linens, with bows on the back of every chair. The dinner was a five-course meal, preceded by appetizers and champagne. I tried to eat at least one bite of each delicacy. I danced the traditional Romanian wedding dance, the Hora. I danced to one song with Cristian. Because I had not been aware the party would last literally all night, and because we had started drinking at 4 pm and I was not used to this level of partying, I was ready for bed by 1 am. Andrei tucked me in and returned to the party. He joined me in the early morning hours, and Cristian, who partied all night, slunk in at around 7 am. I was already gaining consciousness for the day as he came in. I sensed every gorgeous motion of his body as he lay down inches away from me. When I felt sure he was settled, I opened my eyes to look at him. He was still awake, staring right back at me while the morning sun poured in through the skylight. It was the closest our faces had ever been. Then he shut his eyes and presumably went to sleep.

I got up and went to find a bus station to take me back to the city. I was picking up a friend from London and heading to the Romanian seaside with her. Cristian called me later to see where I was. He sounded somewhat astounded that I had made it out of town on my own. Perhaps he didn't know me well after all since he was unaware of how well I could work a public transit system.

My friend and I had a fabulous time on the shore of the Black Sea. There were beach lounge chairs, bright umbrellas, iced cocktails, and loud party music. We wore large sun hats and not enough sunscreen. It was a completely different atmosphere from the cold, windy, rocky

Oregon Coast I had grown up visiting. We met a Canadian and a Scottish man in our hostel and formed a native English speakers alliance. We joked and communicated easily. We were not romantically attached, but when the weekend ended, I invited them back to stay at my large company apartment, where I was otherwise alone. They accepted, and our merry troop continued to party in Bucharest for another couple of days.

I told Cristian all about it when the weekend was over, and I went into the office. I was still in the unfortunate habit of telling him every detail of my life. I wanted him to know everything about me, even though he had already started using it to put me down. My seaside stories made him frown.

"If you had a Romanian boyfriend, he wouldn't like you coming home from the seaside with strange men," he said.

I looked at him. Was he still in love with me? Was he trying to insinuate he could be my Romanian boyfriend? I was now too afraid of who he was and how he treated me to jump into the emotions I felt for him. I brushed off his comment instead of saying something cheeky like, *If I had a Romanian boyfriend, I would hope he would be at the seaside with me!* with a suggestive wink. There were apparently many things we refused to say to each other. There was so much pain in the relationship that I could hardly bear it. I definitely couldn't communicate clearly with him.

All young, wild, and free Romanians had tickets to a 4-day music festival in the majestic Carpathian mountains, and I was going, too. I went with my new friend, Emilia, who had fatefully taken my tour to Niagara Falls when I was an American tour guide. Cristian and Andrei went with a group of friends from work.

I spent most of my time at the festival wondering whether and when I would catch a glimpse of Cristian in the crowd or get to spend time with him and my work colleagues. The only way to categorize my attraction to him at that point was an obsession. Rationally, I had talked myself out of marrying him, but emotionally, I was locked in the firm grip of love intoxication. Even though he broke my heart, I thought about him constantly.

My job at the company had even fewer parameters than before. I was supposed to teach the HR manager to speak better English, but I wasn't teaching all the departments as I had been before. Also, although I was living in the company apartment, I wasn't being paid. I finally realized they would never get me a visa as well. I began to look into going to graduate school in order to stay in the country.

Emilia told me about a website where I could advertise English lessons as a private tutor. I would need to earn money to live on my own. I signed up. The day I got my first tutoring student I went out with Cristian and Andrei. I announced to them that I was leaving the company, moving in with Emilia, and staying in the country on a student visa.

Cristian looked miffed. "Who is going to teach us about the schwa?" he said, referring to our accent reduction lessons.

"We can still hang out," I said. I wondered if he understood that this meant the company rule prohibiting us from being together would be moot. I couldn't make any sense of his disappointment that I wouldn't be working there.

Andrei proposed a toast, and we drank.

Inevitably, as we were supposedly enjoying each other's company, though I'm no longer sure what prompted it, Cristian dropped the accusatory bomb that I was "two-faced." I once again shut down and perhaps only imagined his triumph at my crestfallen face. *What could I say?* I didn't understand what he even meant. I didn't belong to this culture, I came from a completely different place. All I could do was try to navigate being myself while learning how to be in his culture. I had (and have) at least 1,000 faces. This person, who had previously been so kind to me, taken care of me, and reassured me when I made cultural blunders, no longer had any patience for me.

With my time at the company ending, I decided it was time to get to the bottom of things with him. At 7 pm on a Wednesday, I texted him.

Hey, I was just wondering why you said those mean things about me. They really hurt my feelings. I had been trained that this was the best way to express emotions to someone.

Why do you care? he wrote back, *they're just my thoughts, you don't have to believe them.*

I care because you're my friend, I wrote, *I care what my friends think of me.*

Well, maybe you have enough friends. He responded.

Then he unfriended me on Facebook. I downed a glass of red wine and then cried myself to sleep. We were stone cold to each other in the hallways at work, ignoring each other in groups, until Saturday, when I went to the office in the afternoon, knowing he would be there alone. He smirked as I entered his office.

"Are you done being mad?" he asked me with a Cheshire grin.

I was floored. "What do you mean?" I asked. He was the one who had lashed out and unfriended me. He had looked over my head when I passed him in the hall. I was so confused.

"Are you done being upset about Wednesday?" he asked.

"I mean, yes, I don't really know," I murmured, still fairly unsure what was happening, but I felt that Cristian wasn't mad at me anymore.

We chatted about the situation a bit. He had been out with a friend drinking on Wednesday and didn't want to have a conversation about how he was treating me. He also offered that he felt I had done drugs at the festival, and that irked him. I assured him I hadn't, but he didn't seem to believe me. I sat for a while, examining the wall while he worked. My body was paralyzed. So much pain and love for him were all passing through me. My mind was a cloud of emotion, but my body was frozen. With him, I seemed to always be on trial now, I no longer sensed his previous admiration, yet he seemed comfortable saying things to me as if my actions reflected on him and mattered deeply. He cared enough about me to criticize me.

I knew beyond a doubt that I could not change the course of my life to be with a man who was so petty and unsafe. But emotionally, I was burning for him. It was a passionate stalemate.

Intoxicated Attachment

You may experience, or you may have previously experienced, romantic intoxication. These are emotions so strong and compelling you feel you love him and no other. You must have him. Nothing matters except him and his love for you.

These attractions are exciting, except when they are devastating and worse when they are abusive. This is not a loving relationship; this is romantic intoxication, a state similar to addiction. Chemically, attachment to another person works like addiction. Their presence causes a huge dopamine surge in your body. When you are not near them, you experience withdrawal from your dopamine fix of relationship with them. When you do not share an emotional connection, relationships become intoxicated attachments because all the emotions are happening inside of you without the other person joining you in the experience of connection. Your experience of the relationship will be codependent rather than interdependent.

The antidote to intoxicated attachment is true emotional connection. You must build emotional trust with your dates. You build trust through emotional communication and instances when a man promises or agrees to something and delivers. You will know you have emotional trust when you can be your relaxed self around them, receive support from them, feel connected to your own body and emotions around them, and be okay if you appear imperfect in front of them, physically and emotionally. Practice your feminine energy.

When you are unable to experience the best of yourself and the best of another person, you are not in relationship equilibrium. At worst, you are in a living nightmare. Like me, you may have placed a man so high above you that you shrink and shrink and reduce yourself until there is nothing left of you around him. Acknowledge the times you may have fallen into romantic intoxication, and be aware of your tendency to create a similar attachment in the future. Focus on the state of the emotional connection rather than how much your dates like you.

The End of the Party

Within a month of deciding to leave the company, I was registered for a graduate program in International Business Management at the top economics school in Bucharest. I moved in with Emilia, and I was tutoring two very committed students in English for 10 hours each week. Everything had worked out seamlessly. Except I was still hopelessly in love with a man I no longer saw every day. I decided it was time to try the one strategy I hadn't employed. I would confess my feelings to him.

I called my best friend from college to psyche me up. She had already been in a 7-year relationship. She didn't mess around. We hung up, and it was time for me to call Cristian. I paced back and forth. I breathed quickly in and out like a woman about to give birth. Ok. I pressed Call on my phone. Too late to back out now.

"Hello," Cristian answered, "Alana, how are you?"

"I'm good," I said, though I was not at all good, and the way I choked out the words must have made that clear. "How are you?" I asked, attempting to regain composure.

"I'm okay," he said.

It wasn't a lot to go on, but I had my purpose, and I had to put it on loudspeaker before I chickened out. "Listen," I said, "I know it's been a long time, and a lot has happened, but I just need you to know that I still really like you."

He chuckled softly and went silent. I waited with the fist of my free hand clenched tight.

"You know, my grandma just died. I don't really feel like partying," he said.

This hit me in all kinds of ways. I was a bit shocked, and sorry he was experiencing loss, but also I felt like his answer came out of left field, and I hadn't intended to communicate that I wanted to party.

"Oh, Cristian, I'm so sorry for your loss." I recovered emotionally by taking the focus entirely away from myself.

"It's okay," he said softly. Then, he began to ask me some insignificant questions. I knew his family was important to him. I just couldn't figure out what was going on behind the walls of stone I suddenly realized existed around his heart.

After what seemed like a polite amount of time, we hung up with him saying, "Thank you for calling. Maybe when I feel like partying again, I'll let you know."

"That would be great," I said, even though his words did not communicate what he felt for me beyond that I was not a current priority. I felt a little lighter after being honest with him, even though I knew for certain that I would never be with him.

Men With Emotion

By and large, men are less connected than women to the emotional experience of being human. There are both cultural and biological reasons for this, and it is, of course, not true across the board. However, my clients and I have often harbored stories about men lacking emotional capacity, being unwilling to be honest about their feelings, and unable to communicate emotions in a healthy way. I fully accepted Cristian's public verbal abuse toward me as his way of processing emotion. But I did not ask him to do better. I waited around for months allowing him to treat me poorly.

Ask men to do better. Step one in that process is for you to get better at recognizing your own emotions and emotional patterns. The next step is to use emotional questions from the very beginning of your connection with a man or starting today. This helps them get used to sharing their day-to-day emotions with you. With the trust that is built up through emotional communication, you will feel safer asking for clarification about how they are feeling, behaving, or speaking with you when things feel tense. The goal is to create a relationship dynamic where your man's emotional state is respected *and* where you stick up for yourself if the way he communicates with you is hurtful. If he is not sorry about hurting you or feels justified about hurting you in the seduction stage of dating, I will be honest, I don't think he's the man for you. If he isn't willing to be truthful about his emotions, to clarify his words for you when you are confused, or if he shuts down when you share your emotions (provided your emotions are not thinly masked criticisms of him, by the way), then proceed with caution. These are unhealthy emotional responses, and it may be best to walk away. It's so much easier to leave in the early stages of dating. It isn't relationship failure to do this; it's simply emotional incompatibility. There are other women out there who can meet him where he's at, and there are men out there who can meet you at your level.

You do not need to feel that you are a complete master of your own emotions before you can be a great seductress and have a great relationship. You simply need to be willing to practice sharing parts yourself and taking in the emotions of another person without letting them dump all over you, affect you, or crush you. Practice staying connected to your own feminine being and emotions in regular conversation and when conflict strikes.

Having a healthy emotional dynamic can start with you. Changing one side of a connection can shift a whole behavioral relationship dynamic. We started the work of this book with the foundational energy shifts of being and receiving for a reason. Before you do emotional work with another person, you must get in touch with your own presence and your own being. Become aware of how you are being around someone, so you can tell if they are someone who makes you feel emotionally safe or dysregulated. Breathe deeply around people who take you away from your center. Become aware of when you are giving and when you are receiving so you can choose which energy to use and when. Become aware of what kind of treatment you are receiving from your dates, so you know what to accept and to whom you say "no, thank you." Take on a can-do attitude around showing up in emotionally healthy ways on your side.

In my story, I got lost in trying to figure things out without letting the emotions play out. It was me running back to Cristian. Me trying to figure out how he felt and how I felt. Me making attempts to clarify things. It was me asking for repair every time he insulted me. And yet, there were only two times when I directly confessed my feelings about him. Once, the hurt I felt at his insults, and second the phone call where I told him I still liked him.

Imagine the same love story, but where I show up with different energy. In that story, I stayed solid in the foundation of my own being rather than waiting for him to confirm he liked me all the time. Imagine I had told him how much I liked him at any given point. The night he told me he'd like to marry me, for example. My birthday when he broke my heart, perhaps unknowingly. The night I returned to Romania and went out with him and Andrei. The wedding, the music festival, the many nights and afternoons we spent out with friends.

Imagine I had asked myself what I was really receiving from him and allowed him to give what I wanted and said *no thank you* to the behavior that hurt me. Imagine I had honored my own physical and emotional responses and acted on them. Imagine I had flirted with him instead of trying to appear put together and serious. What if I had clearly communicated what I wanted, felt, and understood from his words at all times?

Imagine I had maintained my emotional sovereignty and given Cristian space to share his true emotions instead of quietly accepting the pain, anger, and meanness he dumped on me. I'm not saying we were emotionally compatible and would have ended up together, but certainly, my experience of that relationship and heartbreak would have been very different. The tools of connecting to your power center and using emotional communication can change your life.

Your emotional capacity matters when you communicate with potential dates. Let men know what you want, feel, and love. Let them know how you feel about them. Modeling the level of emotional communication you want to experience with a man is the best way to attract a man who communicates at the level you want.

Surgical Removal

It started with a minor pain in my stomach a week after my phone confession to Cristian that I still wanted him. I felt a piercing in my large intestine region just below my ribcage. I stopped my habit of getting a cheese pastry every morning on my daily commute to my first student. I self-diagnosed myself as suffering from stomach inflammation and went on an anti-inflammatory diet: no more white flour, no more coffee, no alcohol, and no sugar. There was very little I still consumed.

I lost weight first and then my strength. A month passed, and the slight pain had not resolved from my diet change, but my vitality was slipping away. I walked home feebly from class as the days grew colder, and the wind blew so hard it threatened to tip me over. One day after a shower, I fainted, at which Emilia insisted that I go to the doctor, scheduled the appointment for me, and accompanied me to the clinic.

The nurse did an ultrasound of my stomach. She swished the wand through the cold, wet goo on my belly. I lay there looking from her face to the screen, unable to understand her reactions or how the shapes on the screen related to the inside of my body. Finally, she went to get a copy of the scans, handed them to Emilia, and said we needed to see the surgeon at the hospital immediately. We sat quietly in the surgeon's waiting room for an hour. Eventually, he called my name, and we went into a large white room with a desk and a medical exam table. He motioned for us to sit opposite him at the desk.

He spoke English and began to tell me about my scan. It was inconclusive. It was inconclusive because there was an infection the size of a tennis ball inside my stomach, swallowing up my appendix. My other stomach organs had inflamed and twisted themselves around the infection to keep it from spreading. The inflammation made it hard to tell what was happening in my stomach. They couldn't say for certain whether my appendix had already ruptured or not.

"You need to check into the hospital right now. You may be dying," the doctor stated.

I stood up and walked across the room to an exam table, sat down, and began to cry.

"Why are you crying?" he asked emphatically.

"I'm 6,000 miles from home, and you just told me I might be dying!" I retorted through my tears, not even bothering to translate miles to kilometers so the European man could understand me.

I had been in Romania long enough to know that when someone gives you a hard time, it is culturally appropriate to give it back to them. I had been struggling with that aspect of the culture because my original socialization had taught me to do exactly the opposite. I had learned that you should be righteous and composed in public. You should always be polite to authority figures like teachers, police, and doctors. If you don't have anything nice to say, don't say anything at all. It took a year in Romania and the threat of death to convert this nice little girl into someone who spoke raw, unfiltered emotions to an authority figure.

Of course, I was not thinking about that at the time. I was terrified out of my mind. I was so afraid to die that I did something else I was scared of. I checked into the hospital. They hooked me up to all kinds of machines and an IV drip. I was terrified of needles, blood, and any mention of internal organ function. They poked and prodded, undressed me, stuck needles in me, and slid me into a giant white CT scanner. I felt like I was in a science fiction movie. Luckily, they didn't speak English, so I didn't have to understand what they were finding. I always felt sick when American doctors began explaining organ functions to me. I was only told that they had to prepare me for surgery in case they operated that night. That was enough knowledge for me.

Emilia's aunt and boyfriend came to the hospital to be with us. In Romania, when someone needs help, the people gather. They stayed with me until hospital visiting hours ended. I had a nice little room, clean and white, with a view out onto the practice pitch of one of Romania's premier soccer teams. My IV drip was pumping me full of antibiotics, and although I had told the nurses that I had no pain (the upside of so much inflammation), I was given a generous dose of pain medication.

I woke up at 4 am feeling worse than I had ever felt in the entire six weeks of illness. I had to get out of bed carefully, dragging my new wheeled IV appendage with me. It went where I went. Reaching the toilet, I threw up. There was barely anything in my stomach but just enough bile to create a very unpleasant experience. The nurses came to check on me, change out my IV drip, and refill my water. I told them I had thrown up, but they didn't seem concerned. I didn't feel I had the strength or Romanian language skills to communicate to them that this was the first time I had thrown up since I had gotten sick, and it didn't seem right.

I ate a few bites of the yogurt and toast for breakfast. I threw all of it up and continued to vomit the entire day. I felt even sicker and weaker than when I'd arrived at the hospital. The surgeon came in that evening and decided it was a reaction to the pain medicine. I received a new IV, and the vomiting stopped.

The next day I woke up with my right hand swollen up like a balloon. I pressed the call button for the nurse even though it was 4 am. The person who put in my evening IV had missed my vein, and all the liquid was filling up my hand. It was horrifying, but I was beyond emotion at that moment. It might have been the giant dose of drugs I'd received in the previous 36 hours or the sheer sense of loss I felt in my life, stuck in the hospital instead of being at university or work, abandoned by Cristian's love, with no idea whether I would live or die. Fear of the medical establishment deserted me. I felt only apathy toward my giant hand, my whole situation, and the people around me.

The saving grace that day was when the surgeon showed up and gave me permission to eat anything I wanted. I was taken off the awful appendicitis diet and given my choice of the hospital menu. I ate my first real meal in over a month, a yogurt cup, a bowl of soup, some chicken, and most of a slice of bread; I began to feel a bit more whole.

When I woke at my usual 4 am time, emotion crept back in. I felt complete devastation and terror. *This is it*, I thought, *I am really going to die*. Silent tears rolled down my cheeks and I thought, *I never even got to experience being in love with someone*. Then I repeated to myself over and over, *I don't want to die. Please don't let me die*. Which finally turned into, *if I have to die, please don't let it be painful*.

I made it through a week going day-by-day. From 10 am to 10 pm, I had the kindest visitors. Emilia came every day during her free time from university. Her aunt came by a few times with oranges and chocolate treats. Several of my university classmates dropped by, though I'd only known them a month before being hospitalized. Cristian did not visit me nor reach out, which stung somewhere deep in my heart where I tried not to look. Even if he had been the person I felt emotionally closest to in the country, he certainly didn't feel the same way about me.

The surgeon dismissed me after a weeklong stay in the hospital, sending me home with a supply of further antibiotics for a month of bed rest. His idea was to shrink the inflammation down enough to remove the infection surgically without damaging my stomach organs. I set up a sick bed at home. And then, by some miracle, totally arranged by a friend, I met Niall.

I had made friends with the hostel manager where I first stayed upon arrival in Romania. One night, she reached out and invited me to a bar with her and some of the hostel guests. I went for my first post-hospital outing and ordered tea. My antibiotics did not mix well with gin and tonics.

I chatted with some Spanish guests all night, and then I was introduced to Niall at the end. Tall, sandy brown hair, kind but piercing blue eyes, and Irish. We had an easy time talking, falling quickly into the ease of chatting in English with another native speaker. He offered to walk me home since I wasn't staying at the hostel and would otherwise be walking alone.

I was invited out again two nights later with the same group. I accepted. As a shut-in extrovert, I was starving for human contact. We went to a different bar, and Niall and I got to talking right away. At the end of the night, he walked me the extra block beyond where the hostel group was going. We arrived at my building.

"Thank you so much for walking me home," I said.

"You're welcome," he said, turning to face me.

"If you ran," I said, "I bet you could catch up to the others."

He said nothing, and then he leaned down and kissed me. I hadn't been kissed in over a year. I had barely been touched by anyone at all, as Romania didn't have a platonic hugging culture. Niall pulled me in close and held me. I hoped he would never let go.

"Can I come in?" he asked.

Emilia was away, and there was no reason to say no except that I didn't want sex. Would I tell him no, and would it be okay?

I didn't sleep with him. We lay in my bed and talked and laughed. He told me there was no hot chocolate in the world like Irish hot chocolate, and I tried to prove him wrong by making some. I knew he wanted sex, but I was so delicate from sickness and heartbreak, I just couldn't do it. We made out and caressed each other.

He continued to come over on his days off just to hang out with me. I felt incredibly warm and fuzzy around him but very half-alive otherwise. At the end of the month, I went into surgery.

After spending a night in a new sick bed and receiving more tests and IV fluids, I was wheeled into the basement of the hospital and instructed to undress. I took off my hospital pajamas while the female anesthesiologist pushed buttons on a machine, and a male surgical assistant watched covertly from around the corner. I no longer cared about this weird male attention. My body had shrunk down in mass. I looked like a contestant on the fourth week of Survivor. I had been poked and prodded by so many needles and machines I barely recognized my body as my own. I lay down on the operating table, and the world went blank.

I woke up with my underwear gone, my pubic area shaved, and a bloody cord running out of my pelvic area. It was attached to a bag of blood. *What had happened to me? No one had prepared me for this eventuality. Had I been mistreated? What was going on?* I was still in the basement but now in a room full of other people recovering from anesthetic. There were no windows, so I couldn't tell what time it was or how long I had been there. I felt incredibly nauseated. Emilia's boyfriend came in and saw me.

"Alana! You're awake," he said brightly.

"Where's Emilia?" I demanded, quite desperately, though this was a very rude greeting. It seemed I had no more control over what I said or did.

He left the room to get her, and she came running in.

"I don't know what happened," I said, "What is this blood?" I asked, pointing to the drain bag.

I was in a state of pure emotion and need. It turned out my operation had taken five hours, and while they had vacuumed out much of the infection, the whole process necessitated me having a drain bag. When it came time for me to pee, I was too nauseated to stand up and was forced to pee lying down on a tray. That was the end of any physical pride I had left.

It took me over a day to recover from the anesthetic and be able to stand again. Niall came and sat by my side all three of my operation recovery days. He held my hand, and we spoke our beautiful fluid English. His mother was a nurse, he said, so he didn't mind the drain bag lying next to us. I had befriended the nurses during my hospital stays, and the first day Niall arrived to see me, they sweetly changed me into a flowery hospital dress instead of the pajamas I was previously wearing, so I would look good for him. We had a good laugh when I told him why they had changed my outfit because the dress was shaped like an oversized bag.

Two days after I left the hospital, I got on a plane to go visit my family. When I returned to Romania, Niall was already back in Ireland.

Life felt tender and fragile. Inside, I felt slightly numb and absent-minded, which continued for several months as I recovered from the physical wounds of the operation and the many rounds of medication I had taken. My emotional capacity was shattered. I had thought I had sunk as low as I could go, being heartbroken over Cristian. A full year of transition, breakdown, cultural identity crises, heartbreak, and dancing with death irrevocably changed me.

Heavy Emotions

You will likely not feel seductive when you are depressed or sick. Your body will be working overtime to return you to life rather than giving you tasty doses of love-creating potion. Sometimes in life, we don't feel sexy, sexual, or even loving or desiring a connection with anyone but ourselves. These emotional times are also valid. They may happen to you in or out of relationship.

When you are stuck in an emotional (or emotionless) rut, return to your physical energy. Nurture your physical state. That is the key. All of the energetic shifts in this book will support you in returning to equilibrium but especially focus on the physical during times of hardship. Take excellent care of your body. Then apply being rather than doing, receiving rather than giving, and so on. You can attract attention and admiration when in a state of emotional turmoil or numbness, but you may not feel like reciprocating fully. Go slow. Be gentle with yourself.

Later, I would feel some regret for not taking Niall more seriously. At being unable to return his affection because of the sheer emptiness inside me. On the other hand, I was offered a miraculous gift in his attention. For the first time, a man stuck by me when I didn't offer sex in return. For the first time, I followed through on my own desire or lack thereof. This was probably a crucial point in the breakthrough I would have a few years later with feminine energy dating. My desire was the desire that came first.

Exercise: Fearless Emotional Communication

Emotional connection and trust are the lifeblood of an intimate relationship. It is *never* too early to build and rarely too late to rebuild. The sustainability of your relationship depends most on your emotional connection with each other. It governs how you treat each other day to day, and how you repair conflict. Begin by practicing the emotional questioning technique outlined in this chapter. As much as possible, use emotional communication when you speak to men. Masculine people generally relate to the world as an action to take, a problem to be solved, or a puzzle to be pieced together.

When you communicate your emotions rather than a situation or logistics, you communicate relationally. While men will usually listen to you in order to figure you out or figure out what needs fixing, when *you* focus on using emotions rather than facts to communicate, they are better able to hear *you and relate to you.*

It looks like this: "My boss changed our morning meeting structure at the last minute, and it really threw me. I was *confused* the whole way through my presentation, and I *feel* so *embarrassed.*"

He cannot *fix* your experience of confusion or embarrassment, so it will require him to dig deep into his own human experience in order to respond to you. He may react in any number of ways: with empathy, affirming your experience, a hug, or even a joke. If the way a man responds to your experience of the world makes you feel small or defensive, he isn't the best man for you.

You can also use emotional communication to affirm relationship behaviors you enjoy.

"It *feels* so good when you stroke my hair."

"I *love* it when you cook me dinner."

"Dancing with you is my *favorite* part of the day."

The most important time to use emotional communication is in the face of what your body or mind perceives as conflict or potential conflict. This is when you do want to call on the masculine to fix a problem for you. The formula for this communication is simple: Feminine Emotional Statement + Direct Masculine Request = Relational Solution.

Start by speaking your emotions and following them up with a clear request that fulfills your needs or desires. Don't make a man guess what you need. He will likely go into his own trauma around disappointing you, whether he is wanted or worthy, or feel like he wants to withdraw from you if there is uncertainty or what he may perceive as a lack of interest or dismissiveness in your statements. Instead, be direct and clear about your emotions and needs, and allow him to use his masculine energy to create a solution for your needs.

"I had a difficult day at work and *feel exhausted* tonight. Can we meet tomorrow instead?"

Notice the difference between that statement rather than the logistical way we often feel is safer to communicate.

"Hey, something came up, and it would be better if we meet tomorrow. Does that work for you?"

When you communicate emotions alongside your request, you let the other person know how you are feeling, which creates intimacy and understanding rather than uncertainty and defensiveness. Communicating your emotions allows him emotional space to create a logistical solution that works for him as well. His solution could be, "Yes, we can meet tomorrow. How's 7 at the same place?"

Emotional communication also looks like this:

"I'm *feeling uneasy* in this bar. Can we go somewhere else?"

"I don't *feel ready* for sex right now. Do you mind if we take it slow?"

Hot tip: If a match has difficulty meeting your emotional needs at the beginning of dating, this is unlikely to improve with time. Recognize that someone who is resistant to honoring your emotions and meeting your needs is unlikely to be a partner who creates connection and committed love with you in the long run. You can save yourself a lot of time and heartbreak by accepting that your date's level of emotional availability, intelligence, and their own trauma response is not about you. If they can't meet you where you are, it doesn't mean you're a needy, difficult, or unlovable person. It simply means they aren't a good match for you.

TL;DR

1. Keep your focus on feminine emotion rather than masculine logistics when dating.

2. Human bonding is a process of emotional connection

3. Emotional connection is the lifeblood of intimate relationships at the beginning and throughout your connection. Be intentional about creating an emotional connection with dates/lovers/partners.

4. Emotional intoxication is not connection because it is internally focused rather than a shared experience between two people.

5. Experiencing hard or heavy emotions inside or outside of a relationship is normal and okay. Be sure your physical well-being is taken care of at these points.

6. Use emotional communication from your first contact through a committed relationship.

7. Masculine people generally relate to the world as an action to take, a problem to be solved, or a puzzle to be pieced together. Emotional communication is the key to creating a dynamic where you do not feel that you and your life are something to be fixed.

8. Practice emotional communication as often as possible. Bonus note: emotional communication works with all people - not just men.

CHAPTER 9

SHIFT THE PACE

Feminine energy is timeless. It exists outside the bounds of linear time, which is masculine energy. When you date as a feminine person, you want to be in the mindset of timelessness. Timelessness is highly alluring and entrancing because it gives you the ultimate relaxed energy. You are not rushing anything. You are not rushing anywhere. You are savoring every moment, every connection, every person, and every situation. It is the peak achievement of a great seductress. It does not know the bounds of age, appearance, or physical distance. Being timeless is about pure presence.

Become timeless in the general movement of your body and the movement of the relationship. Cultivate an attitude of timelessness around love. Forget what you learned about how many dates to go on before sleeping with someone. Don't base the validity of your connection on how long it takes him to commit to you. Begin to live in a space where you are not burdened by the biological time clock set for you. Your life force energy comes from beyond time and space— date from there.

Timelessness

After illness, the next year of my life passed both slowly and quickly, in weird little spurts and in a long quiet hush of heartbreak. It was like a dream. First of all, I had to rebuild my physical health. My body had shrunk in weight and muscle from months of rest and eating bird-sized portions of buttered toast. I needed strength to live the active lifestyle I enjoyed. I began going out with my graduate school classmates.

I caught the eye of a man in my class, Grigore. We got to talking and laughing, and he invited me to his house for dinner the next week. I knew it was time for me to stop pretending that I wasn't waiting for Cristian and start seriously dating other men. I said yes.

I had to travel out to the middle of nowhere to his house. It was among a small cluster of new cookie-cutter houses built out on an unfinished road. He prepared a fabulous dinner, and we chatted and flirted. We had fun and enjoyed the heady sexual tension. He seemed very confident about his sexuality and honest about his sexual past. He claimed to have slept with 72 women, including a waitress he met at a roadside rest stop. I was put off by this and silently questioned his standards, but I appreciated his transparency. I declined to sleep with him that night, which perplexed him. He protested my departure, but in the end, he let me go (in a taxi, he did not offer me a ride).

I was invited to a party at Andrei's with Cristian and several of our friends. Our friends trickled out until Cristian, Andrei, and I sat solemnly on the sofas and chairs together, just the three of us, like old times. Only now, times were different. Now I had almost died. Now I had a support system in Romania outside of the two of them. Now I knew for certain that no matter how much I loved Cristian, I would never be happy with him.

"Do you remember that conversation we had last year?" Cristian asked.

I immediately knew what he meant—the conversation where he told me he wanted to marry me and build our lives together. Yes, I did. My body went on high alert. My heartbeat quickened, and I stood on edge. Was this the moment I had been avoiding? The one where everything blew up or where he confessed his love for me, and we went off together and lived happily ever after in the sunset? The moment that terrified me?

"Of course I remember," I said indignantly, using frustration as a shield for my terror.

"You remember what I said?" Cristian asked me.

Now I was actually frustrated. Had we not been through months of calling, texting, drama, denial, and dysfunctional behavior, followed by my phone confession and his disappearing from my life? And now, he seemingly wanted to tie this situation up with a bow in front of Andrei. I was very upset.

"How could I forget?" I said softly, trying to keep calm. I was worried about what the two of them were thinking and feeling.

What I felt like doing was screaming at him for saying things that made me believe he loved me and then calculatedly smashing my heart and self-esteem. What I wanted to do was break down and cry over my broken dreams. Instead, I ignored my body, emotions, and all the chaos inside me. In my rush to stay in control, I replied in a lackluster, thoughtless way. Andrei sensed the tension and attempted sarcasm.

"Umm, do you guys need to go into the bedroom and work something out?"

Cristian and I both protested, talking over each other.

"Okay, okay," Andrei put his hands up in a gesture of surrender.

The matter was finished almost as quickly as it had begun.

A few minutes later, Cristian announced that he was calling a taxi to go home, and I did not offer to leave with him. Perhaps I was too afraid of what would happen if we were alone together again. I didn't know what I would say or what he might say. I couldn't risk it. There was no more safety and emotional connection between us, so I awkwardly hung back with Andrei and chatted with him until I felt an appropriate amount of time had passed and I could take my own taxi.

If I had slowed down and taken a breath at any point, the end of that story, and our story, might have been different.

Slow Down

The most useful application of timelessness in feminine dating is to slow down. Really, slow down. The slowness can be applied to everything. Slow down your first impression. Make eye contact and savor it like the first lick of summer vacation ice cream. Relax into your physical movement on dates. Stroll leisurely toward him. During dinner, lift the fork slowly to your mouth. Forget about calculating the rate at which you respond to texts. Respond when you want to and have time to consider yourself, him, and the connection. The speed at which you reply or not is not what determines the strength of your connection. When your date brings up an issue or when you are about to dive into a difficult conversation, slow down and breathe. Take speed out of the equation.

You know the phenomenon that when you worry about giving a fast and witty answer, you are less likely to give a fast and witty answer? The same principle applies to every instance of dating. When you remove speed from your priority list, perfect timing can happen naturally. Apply this, especially to masculine structures like commitment. Let go of your timeline regarding how quickly a man chooses exclusivity with you, commits to you, or proposes marriage to you. Allow yourself to live in timelessness around those structures. Focus on experiencing love at the moment rather than getting your love to a certain level on a specific timeline.

This can feel daunting, especially to my clients who believe they are reaching the end of their childbearing years. So here is some reasoning. The less concerned you are about getting a man to commit to you, the more space you leave for him to be concerned about getting you to commit to him.

If you're taking up all the energetic space wondering, *where is this relationship going? When is he going to commit?* You don't leave room for him to wonder and solve that problem by asking you for commitment. You also kill the attraction because you are deep in masculine energy

- in your head, trying to figure it out logically and forcing structure onto the relationship. Imagine how quickly he'll want to commit to you if the experience of being with you is timelessness, flirtation, and sensuality. The answer here is… quickly.

A good rule of thumb is to be wary of instances where you feel urgency. If you are in a rush, you are not in timelessness. If you feel you need him to text you *right now*, ask you out *now*, and commit to you *now*, you are likely in a trauma state of mind and not in connection with your personal sovereignty and wholeness. If you feel urgency creeping in, use this protocol:

Step 1 - Get back to being. Breathe deeply. Check in with your physical well-being.

Step 2 - Do something you love. Get back to personal sovereignty. Re-focus on your own fabulous life.

Imagine if I had slowed down just long enough with Cristian to realize that being honest about my feelings didn't mean I had to marry him. What if I had just focused on how much I wanted him and loved being near him and allowed myself that experience in the moment? What if I had moved slowly enough to remember that commitment, marriage, family, and happily forever after don't all happen in the same instant? Imagine the conversations and honesty and clarity that would have been created between us if I had slowed down and gotten timeless. I cannot overstress the power of slowing down in dating. Every chance you get, slow down and breathe.

Fast Forward

Because here's what can happen. When a man senses you have no agenda, attraction, and tension will build. He will want you to be his when he sees the confidence and sensuality you embody. He can choose you on date #1 if the emotion is right. That's why I use the word timeless instead of slow. Attraction and commitment are timeless. Some people get married a week after meeting. Others spend years getting to know each other and building lives together before officially committing.

There are no rules. You have to choose for yourself.

Get your deepest desires vision from Chapter 1 back out or create a new one. Re-presence yourself to what *you* want—date for your vision rather than for a specific man. Allow yourself spaciousness and timelessness in finding your ideal partner. Make sure you aren't waiting on someone. Waiting for a particular person to be ready to love you will stagnate your sexual energy. Go slow, sure, but don't put your search for love on hold for someone. When you move without hurry, you will be amazed at how fast real, exciting, fulfilling love can find you. Slow things down so they can speed up.

Choice Is Your Birthright

I'm unsure where I learned that waiting for a man to decide how he felt about me or love me was a good game. But somehow, I learned it and played it over and over. I did not realize that playing that game was my choice. This is your invitation to make choices consciously by remembering you *always* have a choice in the game you are playing.

We make choices every day in dating without realizing that we've made a choice. It's an automatic nervous system response. I often chose to invest time in men who had wavering masculine energy. But the truth is, men who weren't excited to *do* things to get to know me, didn't want to know me. Men who were *indirect* about what they thought and felt about me weren't going to decide they loved me if I just stuck around long enough. In case you recognize yourself in those patterns, I feel you. But I'm here to say it is a *choice* to hang out and wait for a specific man to choose you. Whenever you feel a need to prove yourself to a man or wait for him, don't forget that that's a choice you're making. If you're going to stick to your guns and hold onto a dating connection even though it makes you unhappy, make sure that's a conscious choice.

Parental investment theory is a popular concept espoused in mating science around the differences in how men and women date. The basic idea is that women care more about finding committed relationships because the result of sexual relations for females is pregnancy, which means a minimum 9-month commitment, followed by nursing. This is an interesting explanation for why women care so much about being *chosen* and finding long-term commitment. I'd like to present another theory that I find intriguing - the female choice theory.

This theory centers on hidden ovulation in human females, meaning that women don't have any outward signs of fertility, unlike apes whose bottoms swell and redden or birds who sing mating songs. No one besides a human female can tell when she is physically ready to conceive a new life (and even she only knows if she's in tune with her body's cycle). Historically speaking, there were no children without the act of sex, so the man a female chose to sleep with during ovulation was very important. That man got his genes passed on. In a prehistoric world of natural order rather than the societal order of marriage, the fate of human DNA presumably lay with females. Sexual choice is the biological birthright of women. Don't give away your power by pretending you don't have a choice and settling for less than you desire.

Choose the relationship and sexual experiences you want, and don't accept anything less. Don't ask a man to change. Keep dating until you find what you are looking for. You may have to let go of a good man or two because he is unwilling to create the life you want, it's true. You will be more seductive to all people if you stay committed to your own desire rather than attached to a specific dating relationship. Choose yourself first. Use your power of choice intentionally around dating, commitment, and relationships. And before you make any important choices, slow down and breathe.

Unintentional Choices

After that evening with Cristian and Andrei, I went back and slept with Grigore. I made the decision with my head rather than my body or emotions. It wasn't desire that moved me to say yes to sex, just the thought that it had been too long since I'd had sexual contact and the hope that something might be different with Grigore. All his boasting about his sexual prowess was unfortunately lost on me. I got very little pleasure from being with him. Was I still emotionally and sexually dead inside? Possibly.

A French exchange student joined our class, and we found out we had a common interest in Latin dance. Our interest turned out to be an obsession, and she and I began to go out dancing almost every night. Each night was a different club but the same dancing for hours until our feet swelled out of our strappy dance shoes. Slowly, through her friendship and the sensuality of dance, I was coming back to life.

Grigore did not ask me out on more dinner dates, but he did suggest an afternoon meet-up at my house during his lunch break. He only wanted me for sex, it was very obvious, and I was finally aware I didn't want to settle for mediocre casual sex. I ended things with him very quickly.

"I don't think it's going to work," I said.

"You don't think what's going to work?" He responded in classic Romanian sarcasm. In Romania, sexual relationships are not about work.

"Us," I said, "together."

"Like us as a team?" He said teasingly.

"Yeah," I said, "like us as a team."

Instead of worrying about men, I went dancing—dance, dance, dance.

I met David out dancing. He didn't speak English, but he was handsome, kind, and solid. He didn't mind my awful Romanian, and although my words often made him smile in a quiet, secret way, he never made fun of my speaking.

He asked me out to the movies, so we didn't have to talk much. Creating emotional intimacy was not yet on my radar, so I didn't think anything of it. I was not making intentional dating choices yet. We went on movie dates about once a week, and again, after one month, I decided to sleep with him. Our sex wasn't especially sensual, connected, or great for me, but it felt like the right timing. After all, he was such a gentleman. Dating him was comfortable and comforting. Perhaps I was interesting, exotic, and desirable after all.

But after three months, he told me he didn't have time to see me anymore. He needed to focus on work and school. I accepted our end gracefully and numbly. Then two months later, he showed up at our favorite dance club with an absolutely stunning dancer at his side. She had the face of a model with a captivating hourglass frame. Suddenly, I felt the true sting of rejection. Once again, I was someone's second choice. This time it didn't even feel like a surprise that he would reject me; it felt like it was the natural outcome. I was swimming in a sea of dating pain and heartbreak.

My mother came to visit. We took some trips around the country, taking in the beauty of the Romanian countryside that contrasted the ruinous dirt lodged in all the cracks of Romanian cities and the garbage piled up on the sides of the road. We spent our time in unneglected places, the charming, medieval downtown of Brașov and the lush banks of the Danube Delta, where the river fingers out into the Black Sea.

We returned to Bucharest on the late evening train, slowly meandering our way through mountains and meadows as darkness fell. The train smelled faintly of fuel and the dust of thousands of travelers. I sat facing my mother at a small plastic table where people had stuck their discarded gum and smeared greasy fingers. I checked Facebook on my phone. Cristian was in a relationship.

Reading the words, my heart experienced the physical pain of breaking. I could not help but clutch at my chest. More than a year had passed since I thought we had any chance of being together. I thought my heart was already broken beyond repair, but here it was, physically aching like heartburn. I stared out into the blackness beyond the train window, but all I saw was myself in the reflection, looking right back. A few silent tears streaked down a face I tried hard to love when I couldn't seem to find a man to love it. Holding the ache in my chest, I wiped my face dry and let the train take me home.

Healing

Like relationship building, heartbreak lives in timelessness. Grief is timeless. It never goes away; it simply changes. Healing is also timeless. Whenever I cry or grieve something, I can still feel the pain in my chest that was activated that night. I no longer feel connected to Cristian in any way. I'm fairly certain I never really knew him. Heartbreak doesn't care what happened to you or between you and another person. When you love and lose, whether it's a person or a fantasy, you will suffer. This suffering can feel excruciating; it can make you feel numb. It comes and goes. And then there is a non-timebound point when your heartbreak brings clarity and the opportunity for a new way of being and doing. And all the time, healing is happening.

After my heartbreak over Cristian, time marched on. I worked, I joined an Acro-bachata troop, I went out with friends, and after another celibate year, I started dating Constantin, the tall, dark, handsome man I told you about at the very beginning of this book. It was, as you read before, an intellectual sort of relationship that brought me to tantra and relationship theory. By studying the science and art of mating and dating, I began to pick holes in how I had approached love up to that point and allowed myself to heal.

Slowly, my expectations of love unraveled. Just as I did with Constantin, I expected my dates to know how to love me without being told, believing my ideal man would simply *know* instinctively how to love me. I had been let down each and every time after failing to communicate my needs and desires. In my healing process, I learned that the way people experience and understand love is different, so in order to love someone well, you must learn what makes *them* feel loved. In order for someone to love you well, you usually have to *teach* them. You don't always have to tell them explicitly; your energy and behavior also teach people how to treat you. But direct, structured communication is the most streamlined approach for receiving the love you seek from men.

Time and again, I had hidden my desire from the very men I hoped would want me. Now, I learned to speak in desire. I invite you to experience the healing power of speaking your desires to men. What I used to do and now observe clients doing in dating is to criticize a man's behavior to get him to behave differently. Women show me their dating texts where they chat things like, "I'm not trying to have a pen pal. Are we going to talk on the phone sometime?" This isn't charming *or* relational; it's defensive and may even be controlling. The desire to control is your fear response, so there is no need to judge yourself if you recognize that behavior. Heal yourself by getting into desire in the future. Ask for what you want or tell a man what you would love. You will get a much different response, and you will heal your dysfunctional connection habits at the same time.

'*You have such an interesting take on life. I'd love to talk on the phone and get a bigger picture of your thoughts,*' will go so much further than the previous example. As a bonus, you automatically create emotional intimacy and a relationship by sharing what you want honestly and openly. Using honest, non-defensive communication is essential for a relationship that goes the distance. At all times, speak in desire instead of defense. Tell your dates what you want and how to love you without telling them what to do or insinuating that they're bad or wrong if they don't do what you want. By learning to communicate this way, you create connection, and you heal yourself.

I reflected on the way I had always waited for love, accepting what came around and holding onto it tightly because its appearance seemed fateful to me. Every time I was left thinking *this is it*. No, okay *this* is it. Okay, *this is it*. I perceived love as finite and boundaried. I falsely believed that once you have labels, like exclusive, committed, or married, then you have real love. I gained clarity around the way I had perceived the timeline of love and how long it took to create attraction and love. I previously thought one month was the right amount of time to decide whether you were compatible, and three months was the right amount of time to commit. I let that timeline go.

I saw the way that I had frozen up each time I needed to speak important truths. I saw the blocks of ice around my heart that kept me from opening up to any man and in a way - anyone - until Cristian came along, unfreezing me and turning me into a fragile being. For all the drama of our short connection, he turned me into someone who cried in front of others. Someone who could get sick and die. Someone mortal who just wanted to be loved. It felt safe to be unknowable and unknown, but what I wanted more than anything was to be seen, heard, and loved. He had broken my heart, but he had also broken me open to be able to receive love.

Mirrored to me in Constantin's aversion to sleeping with me was my own sexual shame. I noticed the things I had been willing to do and say to him and the things that I hadn't. I had to stare down the monster of my belief that in order for Constantin to really love me, he had to sleep with me. At the very end, just before I left Romania, I came to the understanding that his not sleeping with me was just about him; it was not at all a rejection of me. This was an incredibly healing revelation, and it clarified for me that it was high time to leave him and pursue the relationship I deeply wanted.

In the study and practice of feminine energy, I found the aspects of myself that I rejected and abandoned in dating - the being, the receiving, the emotion, and the timelessness. When I looked to the future, I had hope that dating could go differently. I was ready to experience a new paradigm in love, one where I was confident, loving, and felt adored and cherished. I was in the process of healing, and I was ready to date from my feminine energy.

Exercise: Moving As A Great Seductress

Imagine a great seductress. Any highly attractive woman will do, including yourself. Imagine her walking toward you. Notice how she moves.

Here's my best guess for what you see in your imagination: The way your great seductress moves is slowly and intentionally. She is powerful, knows where she is going, and she knows she will get there, but she isn't in a rush. Practice moving the way the great seductress from your imagination moves. If she is moving around in a rushed manner in your imagination, walk in that vision, but do it at a pace you can still be intentional about the exercise. Go ahead, stand up now, or walk to your next destination as a fully embodied sensual being. You are delicious!

You can try this in the privacy of your own home and when you're out walking the dog, going to a grocery store, or dancing in a club. Be timeless and present inside your body. The world will notice.

TL;DR

1. Timelessness is the feminine energy opposite the linear time and space of structured masculine energy.

2. Practice timelessness in all aspects of dating: the practical, the emotional, and the sexual can all be improved by dissolving your attachment to time.

3. By practicing timelessness, you become more attractive. The less concerned you are about getting a man to commit to you on a certain timeline, the more space you leave for him to be concerned about getting you to commit to him.

4. Outside the construct of time, you are already a sensual, desirable great seductress.

5. You have enough time to create the relationship, the family, and the love you desire. Be wary of a sense of urgency in dating.

Urgency indicates a trauma response rather than a true desire for connection.

6. Heartbreak, grief, and healing often exist in timelessness alongside love and attraction. Slowing down and being intentional about healing can help you move through negative past experiences in love (in case you are still processing something and it's blocking you from experiencing fun and love in dating now).

7. Female Choice Theory says that because female ovulation (fertility) is hidden, in a world without monogamous marriage, females choose the continuation of human DNA based on whom they sleep with when ovulating.

8. Be intentional when making all dating choices, and if you are struggling to choose, slow down and breathe.

CHAPTER 10

SHIFT TO PROCESS

The feminine is the energy of process, opposite the masculine energy of initiation. Imagine human conception versus human gestation. The male role is to plant a seed, and the female role is to grow the seed into its own sovereign life. A relationship grows in much the same way. It is conceptualized and then grows into something that has a life of its own. As a feminine person dating, your natural sweet spot is focusing on the process. Consider that being in a relationship *is* a process rather than a checklist task or an end-game goal.

What matters in feminine seduction is how it is *right now*. What does he say *right now*? What does he do *right now*? How is the connection today?

Istanbul

I left Constantin and Romania for Turkey and a new life. The moment the plane lifted off Romanian ground bound for Istanbul, my heart began to feel lighter. A fresh start and a change of scenery can do wonders for heartbreak, especially if you go somewhere incredible. I had fallen in love with Istanbul on a short visit the year before. Its ancient cobbled streets are juxtaposed with cement boulevards and imposing glass skyscrapers. The heart of the city is embellished by the enterprising river Bosphorus flowing out to the Sea of Marmara. The Bosphorus divides the continents of Europe and Asia, and Istanbul spreads out over both continents.

All day long and late into the night, public ferries shuttle passengers between the various shores, and private boats sail and motor up and down the river and out into the sea. At four in the morning, fishermen organize themselves along the lowest bridge and cast their lines into the water below to catch what will be sold at shoreline restaurants during the day. Every daylight hour, different mosques send out megaphone calls to prayer, chanting out sacred words in a mode that Western music abandoned long ago. Istanbul is one of the cities on earth where ancient civilization meets modernity. It has been a refuge for people for thousands of years; for me, it was no different.

It was the perfect time and place for me to practice feminine energy. I began to practice being, receiving, and having an intentional emotional connection with myself and others. I became more involved in being myself. I began to ask myself questions like, *What do I want to do? Where do I want to go? What does my body need?* Previously, I rarely or never asked myself those questions. I had lived my life on automatic pilot, doing what needed to be done based on what other people told me to do.

The whirlwind of closing my Romanian chapter the previous month took its toll. I collapsed in sickness and spent my first two weeks in Istanbul on my friend's couch, watching TV and staring out the window. Then, slowly, I began venturing out, taking walks by the sea and making local travel plans.

The friend I was staying with was leaving a relationship and jumped on Tinder to look for new possibilities. Although I had been wary of online dating, I realized I could test my new dating prowess in a concrete way if I ventured to Tinder. *This is a new process - I'll try it as an experiment.* I created my profile.

Online Dating

Today, over 50% of Americans have used an online dating app, and over 20% of current marriages started as online matches. Online dating can be a fabulous tool, but, like any dive into intimacy, it may also stir up your dating triggers and cause you grief.

Here are some tips I used to make it an enjoyable and successful experience rather than intimidating or awful.

1. Treat it as an experiment (meaning get into the process!) - use the dating platform that sounds most interesting to you, or use several of them at the same time if that excites you. Choose everything as an experiment: photos, comments, and conversation starters (more on this later). You are creating your brand of seduction and can adjust these elements as you go. Your profile doesn't need to be perfect.

2. Use current photos - your goal is to show your *being* accurately. You can use your best or favorite photos, but have them be as current as possible. Personality matters, and while you hope to click with a match when you meet, give them an accurate picture (literally) of what you look like. It is difficult to build trust with someone if your first act in the connection is to deceive them. Have a friend take some fun and sexy photos of you if you don't have any recent shots. I suggest using a spread of photos of your profile: a picture of your face, a full-body image, and at least one of you doing an activity you love or in a special place. I also highly recommend having at least one photo/video of you that is sexy or could create sexual tension. When I matched with my husband, my profile included a video of me swiveling my office chair slowly to face the camera with a naughty little smile on my face. It is the top thing he remembers about my profile.

3. Swipe/search from your dating desire. Choose people who match what you are looking for and who intrigue you, and don't waste your energy on those who are incompatible with you or what you want. Wasting energy includes complaining about how many bad profiles you've seen, how many men match you and don't chat with you, and how many people just say, "hey," or have poor chat skills. Let them be. They are probably recovering from a nasty breakup or are just feeling lonely at midnight. Do not waste your energy trying to figure out what their deal is. You have better things to do, like using your energy to search for an actual, compatible, hot-fire match.

4. My genius fellow-dating-coach friend, Amy Palatnick, used this question to determine romantic potential from a dating profile photo would I kiss this person? Your body knows your actual level of attraction to a profile. If you're not sure about a match, ask yourself the question.

5. If you're not having fun while searching, you are probably out of alignment with your great seductress self. Take a break and spend some time reconnecting with your body, your being, and your desire for a relationship before you go back in. How can you make dating app searching fun?

6. Be aware that sometimes searching for what you really want may take more reading and swiping than you think it "should." Enter into timelessness around your search.

7. If starting the conversation is up to you (hello, Bumble), initiate with a flirt. A great seductress knows she is out to find a loving partner and wants to charm him, too. Whatever your first line is, let it be flirty. A flirt says: I am interested in you - I want to know who you are. That is all. But it makes a world of difference in the energy of the conversation because it piques the interest level in your match's mind. Everyone appreciates

being told they are attractive. We all love a little flirt. I did not personally use pick-up lines nor have a cookie-cutter opener. That isn't my style. If it is yours, have at it! You are attracting a match who is right *for you*. My initial flirtations referred to something unique about a man's profile or listed interests. I highlighted a commonality, or if I felt extra flirty, I gave him a direct compliment. When nothing flirtatious comes to mind, say anything and add a winky face. "Hello ;-)" goes a long way.

8. As soon as possible, transition into emotional communication, as learned in Chapter 8. The flirtation-emotional connection question system is a micro version of creating sexual tension and emotional connection. You don't need to be on an in-person date to create rapport and learn essential facts about your match. You can check values alignment with a few simple emotional questions. Emotional questions generate more energy in the conversation, and if you really get going, you will stand out from anyone else he is chatting with. He may not know why, but because of the emotional connection, he will sense that *there's just something about you*.

9. When communicating with men, I recommend that you ask only one question at a time. If you like long, letter-style messaging, then please do that. I had several lovely connections with men who enjoyed writing this way, though they did not work out long-term. In general, however, it's best to stick to one topic and one line of questioning at a time during initial dating chats.

10. Above all else, honor yourself and your own energy in online dating. When you aren't enjoying a conversation or someone says something that puts you off, honor yourself first. Check in with your being, your body, and your emotions. Are you in process,

receptivity, and timelessness? Do not agree to dates you don't want to go on. Practice using your masculine energy to defend your feminine desires by asserting yourself at all times. End any connections that aren't living up to your expectations or desires. You will thank yourself when your ideal match does come along.

11. I recommend online dating because it is a surefire way to be presented with people who are single and looking for connection. If you don't like online dating or feel it isn't your style, don't let yourself fall into scarcity thinking around the availability of men. For years I met men at parties, schools, work, dance classes, and hiking in the mountains. Online dating is the most streamlined way I am aware of for meeting eligible and interested partners, but don't let your mind tell you it's impossible to meet someone another way.

New Dating Paradigm

Tinder was my very first online dating experience. I got one Super Like and then no other bites. I agreed to a date with my Super Like since he was the only match I got. I was still in my old habit of scarcity and disbelief that someone might super-like me, so the idea of saying "no, thank you" and trying to meet a different man didn't occur to me. Later, I learned my account had a location glitch, which led to me getting no matches.

I met my Super Like outside his apartment (this was before I decided absolutely no first dates in homes), and we played Backgammon. I am not a huge board game fan, but it was a low-pressure way to get to know someone. He won a game, and then I won a game. He wagered that if he won the next round, I had to kiss him. The sexual tension was set. I was winning up to the end, and then he won. I kissed him, but I could feel that I didn't enjoy it in my body. Although he begged, I declined a second date simply because I didn't want one. I had learned to respect my sovereignty.

I got on Bumble, and my luck turned around. The matches began coming in. I had never had so much male attention. By using emotional communication, I quickly found that most of the men were not worth a long conversation, and I was able to narrow the playing field. I didn't take it personally when my matches fell short. I knew I was looking for someone special, not someone average.

I did not push myself to continue discussions that I felt were going nowhere. I did not help my matches by asking lots of questions to keep the conversation flowing. Instead, I trusted them to use their masculine energy to take action when they wanted to and prove to me that they had conversational skills. I did not exhaust myself trying to speak to people who didn't put effort into talking to me. It was a good match if my attention was on being and creating a flirtatious connection instead of trying to scrape a conversation out of someone. I simply let go of the chat when I saw obvious mismatches in values and desires. I had finally realized that not everyone was eligible to be my soulmate, and rather than blaming myself for being a bad fit, I allowed our incompatibility to be a neutral fact.

For the sake of my own feminine energy, I withdrew focus from any matches or conversations that did not give me life, intrigue, or excite me. Rather than going into mental chatter about why he said this, what he meant by that, or why he abandoned the conversation, I simply redirected my focus onto men who interested me physically and conversationally. I settled on a couple of matches I liked due to their profiles and initial conversation.

I went out for drinks and then a meal with one match and had a lovely, flirtatious, and thoughtful time. Then for our second date, he took me to a private island where it turned out his family owned a home. Entering a private home without having agreed to go there made me feel physically less safe, and when he began demanding sexual favors, I became physically uncomfortable. While I did make out with him and watch him jerk himself off, I did not completely numb out and appease his requests for sex.

Finally, with the weight of his demands and his sexual pressure appeased, I re-engaged with my own feelings of discomfort and unhappiness. I remembered my sovereignty, and I left despite his protests. I found my way back to the harbor alone and figured out the ferry back to the mainland by myself. I stared out at the waves processing the experience mentally, emotionally, and physically. He was engaging and good-looking, and he wanted me. But I wanted to be with a man who respected me enough to put my comfort and happiness before his sexual needs. I simply wouldn't settle for less than that anymore. Beyond that night, I did not waste any more time thinking about him.

Even though I was striking out in terms of great matches, dating had already changed for me because I was no longer disappointed in myself or these men for somehow failing at love. We weren't a great match for each other—end of story. I did not feel anxious, guilty, wrong, or bad about my time with them. I did not spend lots of mental or emotional energy on them.

Then there was Berk. His profile listed him as an International Man of Mystery. He was well-traveled, had great style, and possessed one of the most attractive faces I had ever seen.

'Hello, international mystery man. Who are you really?' I wrote to him, adding a winky face at the end. I did not bother to overthink my opening line. In seduction, the energy matters more than the mental chatter details.

'Ha! I don't really know to be honest,' He responded and asked me a follow-up question.

We hit it off right away. He was the son of a British mother and Turkish father who had been born and raised in Germany and had spent the last several years in Sweden. We had English and German, a sense of split cultural identity, and a deep love of Istanbul in common. We had our first date the same week we matched.

He took the sunset ferry across the Bosphorus to meet me on the Asian side of Istanbul where I was staying. He was tall and lanky, and he moved through the world with a skimming stride. He had a sweet

British accent and spoke in gusts. Over dinner, I mentioned my school days in a small private German system, a topic that had an emotional undertone for me.

"No way!" He exclaimed, 'I went to a Steiner school as well."

We had grown up in the same school system, two continents apart. I had been aiming to reveal an important factor about my upbringing and stumbled upon a place of deep connection for us. The trust between us, and therefore conversation, opened up, and the night became magical.

I had never been on a date like it. I felt safe with him but also intrigued by him. I felt connected to him but not dependent on how much he liked me. I also did not doubt that he was interested in me because of his enthusiasm for speaking with me. I knew I was powerfully centered in my feminine energy. At the end of the night, he said he wanted to see me again and introduce me to some traditional Turkish food. We agreed to meet for lunch two days later.

On our second date, we created more sexual tension and emotional connection. But he still didn't kiss me goodbye. I felt confused and a little impatient with his... was it timidity? Lack of lust for me? I was still trying to interpret what it meant for him not to kiss me, but I didn't let myself make a definitive judgment. I didn't discard him or get weird energetically because of how I was secretly feeling about being unkissed. I trusted that anything that had not been communicated directly between us - his wanting to kiss me or not - was a mystery. So I was able to hang with the tension of being un-kissed. I stayed in the chaos of the unknown.

My friend threw a party for the Tinder man she had been chatting with and several of his friends, and I invited Berk. It was a happy gathering of Turkish and English; the air was thick with flirting and friendship. Berk stayed behind as everyone trickled out, and my friend went to bed.

Then there was no more hesitation on his side. He kissed me softly and then more intensely than I'd ever been kissed. We made out wildly on the couch until four in the morning when we could barely keep our eyes open. It turned out the man was not timid and had plenty of lust for me.

I caught a flight for a weekend trip with my friend at dawn. I couldn't stop smiling just thinking that Berk existed, but I did not obsess over him. I did not try to guess what he was doing every waking hour or check my phone every other minute to see if he had texted. I did not worry about whether he was seeing other girls while I was away.

When I returned, he and I met again on the European side of the romantic streets of Istanbul, where he was staying, and returned to his apartment. I let him pleasure me like no man before, emotionally and physically. I received openly from him without worrying about owing him or proving my worth to him. I relished his touch. I loved laughing with him.

The next morning, I felt peaceful holding his hand as we walked down the street. I stood up a little straighter. I felt fully myself and grounded in my body. When I left him to take the ferry back to my side of the river, I did not worry about how often to text him back or when I would see him again and for how long. I was fully engaged in experiencing my capacity to be myself, receive from him, be physical, emotional, and present in the process of discovering him. And I knew he was captivated.

I did not know about being a great seductress yet, but I was becoming one. I had shifted my dating energy. People around you will notice when you embody high feminine energy, and your dating results will change.

Process Vs. Control

The power of shifting into the process is that it helps you relinquish your perceived control over your date and where the relationship goes. Most of our dysfunctional relationship behaviors show up when we are afraid we have no control, and we attempt to get that control back.

Seductive feminine energy is about the relating process, not controlling the initiation or outcome of a relationship. As I said in the Introduction of this book, seduction is not about manipulation or control; it is about sharing your attractiveness with another person and allowing them the pleasure of experiencing you intimately. It is, in fact, the opposite of control. It is about relating to someone. If you are truly in the process of getting to know someone, you cannot make definite predictions and pronouncements about what the future holds for the two of you. It will become self-evident that you don't know them well yet.

Previously, when the dating process included uncertainty about how much men liked me or where the connection was going, I freaked out. It resulted in behavior like repeatedly texting the man irrelevant messages, spending hours crafting the perfect note to him, or even distancing myself from our connection. In all these actions, I was trying to control the relationship. Rather than getting into the process of *being* in a relationship, I was trying to force a specific response from them. Rather than taking responsibility for myself and my half of the relationship, I was trying to get them to choose the outcome I wanted (a committed relationship) without having to ask for it. I wanted men to choose a relationship with me, so I would try to guess what they were thinking and how I could get them to want me. I then opted for behaviors that led to less attraction. I opted for perceived control.

When I harnessed feminine energy, I stopped worrying about controlling where the relationship was going. I focused on where the relationship was at that moment and the *process* of building a deeper connection. I focused on how I was and what I desired at that moment. I began to measure relationships by my own desires and standards rather than how much men liked me and wanted to commit to me. If a man doesn't want you or doesn't treat you the way you desire, he isn't the man for you.

Period.

Stop.

Point blank.

There is no more straightforward way to say this. If he doesn't want the relationship you want or doesn't treat you the way you want to be treated, it means he isn't the man for you. It does not mean you aren't lovable, that what you want is wrong, or that you could change him into someone who fits your idea of love, given enough time and effort. Get out of control and get into the relationship process. Leave when it isn't the relationship for you.

I had only one month in person with Berk before I left for America to see my family for Christmas, but I did not worry about our dating future. I knew he would write to me as often as he wanted. I knew I could write to him whenever I desired. I knew we would see each other again if that was what we both wanted. Timeless. A relationship process based on desire. I trusted his emotions, and I trusted my own.

I also knew what I was looking for: an intimate, passionate, and committed relationship with a man who wanted to build a family with me. I was not going to force Berk into the husband and father box if it wasn't what he wanted. I was not looking to control his future; I was working to create mine.

I knew I would not stop dating until I found the relationship of my dreams. And I knew feminine energy dating was precisely the process to get me there.

Hot Dates Hot Life

I got back on dating apps in the US to see if feminine energy dating worked in my own culture. I met Dan, a sensitive and introverted man with a dark sense of humor and a passion for life. He loved music, games, and ancient cultures. He was ambitious but laid back. I loved spending time with him and didn't shy away when he told me he couldn't get enough of me. I finally knew I was sexy and intriguing, and it didn't upset me when people noticed. We met in snug coffee shops and classy bars. We took walks holding hands. He gave me a playlist that made me cry and cooked me zoodles for our first at-home date. We had an easy connection with lots of fast talking and laughter mixed in with profound moments of slow conversation and thoughtful contemplation. *And* there was something about our connection that didn't quite satisfy me.

I left my hometown after the holidays to visit my grandma across the country and let things fizzle with him. I was not yet able to do a clean break. I experienced confusion and fear about telling him no, thank you, and allowed him to get the message slowly rather than kindly and clearly ending things. I was wishy-washy instead of powerful with him in the end. I vowed to do better during my next round of dating. But feminine energy was changing my life. I was excited at the possibilities of love building inside me. It turned out I could be wanted. It turned out a man could worship me. It turned out that a sexy and fulfilling committed relationship might be in my future. I allowed myself to believe it was possible.

Connecting to my being was shifting more about my life than just dating. I began to take my life desires more seriously as well. I wanted to return to Europe, and I wanted to spend more time on music. There was a vocal program in Denmark that I could not afford, but that was everything I wanted. As I focused on my feminine energy, I found purpose in doing things I loved, even if I couldn't guarantee a material Return On Investment. I was worth the things I loved, simply because I loved them. So I took a chance and applied for the vocal program despite lacking the funds. Working in Romania had not made me flush by the standards of western countries.

Within two weeks, I was accepted to the program, and I received a credit card with the exact amount of the tuition that didn't need to be paid off for a year. I found a room that cost just slightly more than my rent in Romania, and I accepted an online job translating a museum exhibit on corsets that would pay my bills while I was in school. I was headed to Denmark to change my voice. I was lit up from the inside in a way only people who take chances on what they love can be.

First, I stopped in Romania to see friends and tie up parts of my business there. I stayed with Constantin. Our dynamic was much the same as it had been when I left Romania, but on the third night of my visit, we had sex. I was utterly bewildered. It had been a year since we had first started dating, and then we had been apart for four months. The sex hadn't been my idea, nor did I feel very connected to my body or him during the experience. I went into confusion. I almost didn't want to move or say anything, in case I broke whatever spell was causing him to be ready to be sexual.

Afterward, my mind gave me plenty of reasons why he was suddenly ready - including that I was now simply irresistible because of my feminine energy practice, but instead of getting sucked into my mental chatter as was my previous habit, I stuck to my being and my body. I regained physical presence in my body after our sex. I tended to my own emotions. I thought about the question: *What do I want?* Instead of, *What does this mean?*

What I truly desired was a passionate and intimate relationship with a man who communicated clearly and was all in and committed to me. Constantin and I did not have this dynamic. The next morning, he didn't mention the sex or our future, and for the first time in my dating life, I didn't worry about it. I did not want what he offered, and I didn't pine after him for not offering it to me. We parted on loving friendly terms with our usual unspoken agreements.

I was finally so engaged in making my own desires come true that I didn't spend my time worrying about what a man felt or thought about me. I didn't worry whether he would write to me or want me back. I wanted myself back. I was ready to experience the best of life, and that energy made me sexy.

Exercise: The Next One Step

Check-in. Where are you right now in your dating process?

Are you still heartbroken over an ex?

Are you afraid to put yourself out there on dating sites?

Are you sick and tired of the low-quality matches you've been getting on dating sites?

Are you going on dates but not having as much fun as you would like?

Are you wondering where your soulmate is?

Write down what it is for you. Now write down where you want to end up.

I want to date loads of sexy and interesting men.

I want to find my life partner and the father of my children.

I want to be in a soulmate relationship.

Now consider: What is the next step you can take from where you are today to where you want to go? It can be a tiny step or a massive step. The choice is yours. Take one step in the process. Today, make just one step toward the relationship reality of your dreams.

If you need help uncovering what that step might be, or if you feel stuck or frozen in place, unable to move in any direction, reach out to me or another relationship coach or therapist. There are countless people out there trained to help you move the needle of your hurt, fear, and any trauma that may be holding you back.

TL;DR

1. The feminine is the energy of *process,* opposite the masculine energy of initiation.

2. The greatest power of shifting into the process is that you relinquish your perceived control over your date and where the relationship goes, and instead put your focus on getting to know who your date is, what they want, and how they love. This kind of attention is attractive to just about anyone.

3. Dating with seductive feminine energy is about the interpersonal relating process, not controlling the initiation or outcome of a relationship.

4. What matters to the feminine in the seduction phase of dating is how it is *right now,* not how it could be *if* and not how it used to be.

5. If your date doesn't want what you want in dating or life, they aren't the right match for you. It doesn't mean anything about you or your worth if the two of you don't have the same desires right now.

6. Online dating can be a fabulous tool, but, like any dive into intimacy, it may also stir up your dating triggers and cause you grief. Use my tips to make it an enjoyable and successful experience.

7. While I don't recommend chasing men, *always* pursue your dreams and passions. Living a life you love will make you more grounded, connected to yourself, and full of vitality, making you a sexier and better partner for anyone you choose.

CHAPTER 11

FEMININE SOVEREIGNTY

You now understand the most potent feminine energy shifts for becoming magnetic, seductive, and desired in dating.

From doing to being.

From giving to receiving.

From thought-based to body-based.

From structured and stifling to wild and imperfect.

From logical to emotional.

From time-bound to timeless.

From control-oriented to process-oriented.

I like to sum up this energetic state as high feminine sovereignty. Maintain that state by:

1. Returning to being. Strategies to bring you back to your own being are breathing, doing things that light you up, and spending time with people you love.

2. Refocusing on what you have received and are receiving in your intimate connections.

3. Refocusing on your physical body. Notice how you are physically at all times during the dating process.

4. Allowing the wildness, even the chaos, of your internal experience of dating to show up, however it's showing up. Be with your wildness without immediately acting on it.

5. Allowing your emotions to be what they authentically are - cry without judgment, laugh without shame. Bring your emotions to the table.

6. Slowing down. You'll notice that when things go poorly in dating, you're tempted to rush to "solve" them, "fix" them, or resolve them by ending things, blocking someone, or ignoring a date. Complete all the other energy shifts on this list before making a move. You'll notice the slower you move in dating, the more entrancing you are. You'll notice that when you don't rush a conversation, sex, or commitment, all these things happen much more comfortably and effortlessly.

7. Noticing where you are in the dating process, and I mean noticing where you really are. Are you dating someone who fits in with your vision or are you kidding yourself? Are things really going well, or are you constantly doubting yourself and struggling? How often do his words and actions match up? How is it right now?

You are not responsible for controlling your date's behavior or determining the exact trajectory of the relationship, but you are responsible for your half of the connection. Being in feminine sovereignty mostly entails keeping your focus on your own energy instead of on what is unknown about your date. When you are not directly connecting with your date, keep your energetic focus on yourself, your being, and your body. Don't lose sight of the fact that you are large and in charge of your life and love. You will achieve feminine sovereignty when you can be, receive, experience your body from the inside out, feel authentically, accept wildness, and get into a timeless process.

All that is left for you now is applying the energetic shifts regularly and watching the magic that follows in your love life.

Chasing The Dream

I moved to Denmark on a bright but blustery day. I had missed a connecting flight, so I arrived just as my first day of vocal school began. I stumbled sleepily into the classroom with all my luggage. In the evening, I took the train to my apartment and found that the cheap room I had rented was about the size of two twin beds side by side. Thankfully, it contained only one twin bed and an upright IKEA closet. The floor space was too small for me to lie down fully to exercise; there was just enough space for me to open my closet and dress. The room had no windows, and the door had likely been kept shut most of the time as the air held a heavy aromatic scent mixed with human body odor. I was essentially living in a closet.

I can do this, I told myself. *I won't be at home very often.*

I had big plans for Denmark. The vocal school was intensive, nearly all day, every day. I intended to dramatically change my voice and vocal habits, spend time with friends I already had in Denmark, and make more. And I was going to continue my research on feminine energy dating.

The first weekend, I skipped town with a friend and headed to the sun-soaked streets of Valencia, Spain. We stayed in a fabulous downtown hostel blocks away from the epicenter of Carnaval. On Saturday night, we made our way down the streets of people laughing and drinking, accompanied by a few new acquaintances from our hostel. We ended up at a large square full of people and action. Colorful ribbons and flags hung from the windows around the square, food vendors were scattered around the street, and party music blasted from the stage speakers. Our group created a small circle in the crowd and danced and cheered right alongside the masses. I felt the exhilaration of boxed wine and celebrating with so many other people.

A woman from our group came on to me. She was married, she told me, but she had an open situation and was interested in me.

It turns out that living in your true feminine energy does not just make you more attractive to men and males. It will make you more attractive in general and across the gender, sex, and sexuality board. As I said before, energy works beyond the labels and boxes humans have designed around love and identity.

Rather than worry about this woman's unrequited attraction, and become embarrassed and stressed out about her confession, I fully owned that I was interesting and desirable. Usually, when someone expressed interest in me which I did not return, I got very befuddled about what I had done to bring about this attraction, and whether I had said something wrong or too suggestive. This time, I accepted that I was hot and seductive. It was not surprising that she found me attractive because I finally understood and believed I was.

This will happen in social situations for you, too when you are practicing feminine energy and personal sovereignty. You will believe in the power of your own attractiveness. I did not experience brain fog or stumble over my words when I replied to her. I simply said that I was incredibly flattered but that, as a rule, I didn't get involved with married people. She accepted that response seemingly easily.

Later that night, I felt a man in our group named Logan dancing close behind me. He was different from my usual type; namely, he was younger than me. He was nicely built, blonde-haired, blue-eyed, and had a bright face with a button nose. His hands were firm, but his dancing was not forceful or invasive of my personal space. I felt in my body that I didn't mind him being so close. Previously, I might have gotten into my head about what it meant for him to be dancing with me. I might have wondered about his intentions and why he had chosen me out of all the women in our group. This time, I dropped fully into my body instead of letting my brain take the reins.

When the show in the streets ended, we headed to a nearby club to continue our celebration.

Logan was an American country boy, whom multiple people in Europe had told that he was the most American person they had ever met, baseball cap and all. Instead of worrying about whether we had matching American politics, values, and life goals, I left my own stereotypes and assumptions about age, politics, and compatibility measures aside, and I focused on having fun and connecting with him as a person rather than a voter or the love of my life. We danced the two-step to some bouncy European pop music and laughed like anything.

Cut to the end of the night where we made out in our hostel bathroom and slept cuddled against each other in the top bunk of a bunk bed. We were wild, free, cozy, and brimming with dopamine and oxytocin.

And I didn't make it mean anything or wonder whether he was the love of my life. I made intentional choices about how deeply to connect with him emotionally and physically. I was not guessing, fantasizing, or worrying about him, me, or us together.

I was fully connected to myself and my energy. I was in feminine sovereignty.

From sovereignty, I was able to trust that my connection with Logan would play out exactly as it best served both of us.

Submissive

In mainstream places where I was learning about feminine energy, I often saw the word *submissive*. Understand that there is no first and second in non-linear, chaotic feminine energy. There is no leader and follower. There is no dominant and submissive. The idea of submission only exists in a linear masculine paradigm. As a feminine seductress with feminine sexual energy, you transcend that paradigm.

You do not need to submit to a man to be powerfully feminine.

There are ways to think about leadership from a feminine perspective. In seduction, you can imagine allowing men to lead in masculine energy areas: structure, doing, logistics, and giving. This generally looks like the masculine partner handling commitment and relationship definition, date planning and implementation, picking up the pen you accidentally dropped, and being the principal giver of time, energy, and money.

You will learn more about your dates, how they respond to life, and what they are capable of simply by letting them lead with masculine energy. It is not that you are incapable; it is that you are curious about what *they* are capable of. So, rather than thinking of yourself as passive or submissive in the dating energetics, think about what you want and need so you can communicate what it is and request it effectively.

I found it incredibly practical and fulfilling to lead in feminine energy areas during dating. This looks like leading with your body, emotions, being, and receiving in the relationship. It means standing where *you* want to and gesturing in ways that feel good to you. It means telling your dates what you love, what you want, and when you feel wonderful around them. You may even let them know your secret feelings, for example, that you think they are amazing, hot, good in bed, etc. Be your authentic self unapologetically, so you give him permission to be his true self, too. Receive as much attention and affection as you can bear.

You may be leading your date to new levels in his own perception of his body and emotions. You may be leading him to be the man he always wanted to be. You may be leading him to give more than he knew he had in him.

Leave ideas of domination and submission for bedroom games. Practice leading in your feminine energy on dates. You will be irresistible.

Nordic Dating

By the time I got to Denmark, I felt confident in my ability as a great seductress.

Men found me attractive. Men appreciated me. Men treated me well, and men wanted to spend time with me. This was now the opposite of my previous experience in which I was not beautiful enough for the kind of man I wanted. I had thought I wasn't interesting or fun enough to keep around for long, and men generally used me and disposed of me.

I now felt calm and even excited when I headed to a dating app, anticipating great connections and feeling no doubt that I could expect fun and sexy experiences from my dating escapades. I had completely obliterated the story that I could only handle one man at a time. I had previously told myself that dating more than one man at a time was selfish, dishonest, and overwhelming. How could you really get to know someone if you also spent time with someone else?

In hindsight, this wasn't solid reasoning for my general social energy. I certainly didn't expect that I could only handle one friendship at a time. That kind of scarcity thinking around energy for intimacy never came up for me in making new friends or meeting groups of new people. My insistence on dating only one man at a time had led me to hyper-focus on a specific relationship panning out the way I hoped it would. It kept me emotionally reliant on how one connection was going in my dating life. It had actually been a terrible strategy for me.

Now I swiped and swiped until I found multiple matches, Jens, Tomas, and Emil, who all had interesting profiles, matched with me, and communicated in ways I liked. Jens turned out to like texting too much for my taste. Eventually, I found myself less and less excited to text him back. In all honesty, I forget what exactly happened to our connection. It was less interesting than the others I was experiencing. I was fully focused on relationships that intrigued me and were heading in a direction I enjoyed. I removed attention from conversations that seemed to be a dead end, people who were boring or who put in no effort right out of the gate, men who didn't ask me out, and anyone who didn't spark curiosity in me.

Tomas was from Norway and pursuing a Ph.D. at a local university. He had ashy brown hair and soft blue eyes that sparkled when he spoke. Our first date was in a small wine bar in a popular neighborhood in the city. It was romanticly lit by candlelight and possibility hung in the air. We hit it off right away. I don't remember the details of our conversation because the connection was what mattered. We smiled at each other, laughed, shared moments of intellectual curiosity, and created a sweet and tender emotional intimacy.

In short, we had a great time.

Emil was a professional football referee. He was tall, blonde, and built like someone who ran back and forth on a field for a living and biked everywhere like a true resident of Copenhagen. He had a slow and steady way of communicating, but underneath he was incredibly goofy and kind-hearted. He had traveled extensively and was into yoga and reggae music.

"I'd love to meet you in person," I wrote to him after a few days of chatting, communicating my real-time desire instead of playing a mind game as I used to do. 99% of the time, this specific text turns into a serious offer for a date. You shouldn't have to convince a man to date you. You simply need to tell him what you want. Emil did not disappoint.

Our first date was in a small bar with lots of twisting hallways creating private nooks to settle in. He got our first round at the bar, and we went off together to search for the perfect corner. It was a weeknight, and the place was mostly deserted. We chose a cozy, cushioned booth and sat next to each other. The conversation was light and fun. His presence had a gravitas, which likely came in handy when he made calls on the football pitch. He gave the impression that he could handle things, including himself. He didn't make me laugh out loud, but we both smiled widely throughout the night.

And then I went home with him. I wanted him, and I wanted to try saying yes to sex purely for desire rather than because it was the right time or the right thing to do.

He lived in a second-floor apartment with high ceilings and a view out to the street. His bedroom was large and modestly furnished with a queen bed, a table, a wooden armoire, and a television in the corner. I stared out the window at bikes whizzing by in the dark street below while he set himself up for the evening. Instead of feeling useless and awkward at this point, I focused on grounding myself by breathing into my point of feminine power. I checked in with my emotional state and made some solid plans for the rest of the evening. He wanted me to spend the night. I felt good about that.

We sat facing each other in his bed, and he played me some upbeat jazzy music.

"Just listen to this," he said admiringly, moving his body to the saxophone's purr.

Then he kissed me warmly and insistently. The music played on in the background. He had the biggest penis I had ever seen. I was pretty intimidated, given my previous experiences with penetration and pain, but with enough lube and foreplay, I felt nothing but pleasure and timelessness. He held me while we slept, and when I left in the morning, I finally understood what it meant to have been fucked and liked it.

Then I went about my day, doing what I needed to do and feeling great about myself. I was not in an emotional tailspin about whether I would see him again and whether he was my entire future. I had had a wonderful night and loved being where I was in life. I was studying the human voice, improving my singing, and spending time with other singers from around the world. I knew at least two men in the same city as me who were fabulous dates. Men in various countries were writing to me. There was no reason to worry about having slept with a tall nordic sex god.

I had never before been a woman men kept in touch with past the possibility of sex. With an emotional connection in the mix, I held their interest beyond physical contact. I loved hearing from all of them. It turned out I did have the energy to enjoy the emotional connection with more than one man at a time. My connections with men lit me up, but I was energetically sovereign and not dependent on masculine attention to feel good about myself. I genuinely loved being myself and experiencing life in my own body. My feminine energy was rising, and my seductive power was at an all-time high.

Logan wrote to me that he was passing through Copenhagen. I told him I was very sorry, my room was the size of a broom closet containing a twin bed, so I couldn't offer him lodging, but that I would love to see him. And he came. We got two more days together, wandering the streets of Copenhagen in the early spring. And we spent a little time alone in his hostel room, messing around without full-on sex. When he left, I knew I would see him again if it was meant to be. He had already proved once that he was willing to travel to me.

The next weekend I met Tomas at a games bar, and he also invited me back to his place. When it rains, it pours, once you have raised your sexual energy. I accepted the invitation to see his living quarters, but when it came down to the moment, I said no to sex. "I'm not ready," I said simply. It didn't feel as easy or desirable as it had with Emil. So I honored my hesitancy and said no, thank you.

And then I saw Emil again. Tall, sturdy, and smiling from ear to ear. We went to a trance dance concert in a building that seemed a lot like a wooden barn and danced the night away before returning to his apartment. He was a very kinesthetic person and I was fully in my body with him. He didn't ask many questions, so I had plenty of quiet space to feel into my being. I was being a thoughtful, slower, relishing, feminine version of myself with him. We were all sweetness and fun. I went home with him again.

The next morning, he was not in a rush for me to leave. He told me about a famous detective show that he said was an important part of Danish culture. The next thing I knew, he was standing next to the television translating every line of a 45-minute episode for me, laughing at all the jokes as they went by. I marveled at him. I didn't leave his house until three in the afternoon.

"See you soon," we both said. But we didn't see each other soon. He stopped writing to me that week. And I was okay because I was fully sovereign in myself and not dependent on men I had met three weeks before.

A month later he wrote to me that he was incredibly sorry for disappearing. His father suffered from alcoholism and had made a suicide attempt. Emil had returned to his hometown to care for his father, and he wasn't sure how long he would be there.

I was very grateful I hadn't spent time worrying about whether Emil didn't like me anymore. I wrote back to him that I was sorry to hear it and that I hoped they were both doing okay. After we texted back and forth a few times, I said, 'please don't worry about disappearing. And I'll probably be back in 6 months, in case things are different for you then. ;)'

And six months later, I heard from him again.

The One

When you are a great seductress, there is only you and the One who is a good match for you. You do not need to worry about beating out other women or being the best date this man has ever had. Those worries only get in the way of your feminine presence. When you think competitively, you are in your masculine energy. Masculine, structured energy moves linearly. Linear means that one is in front of or behind the other, so masculine people thrive on competition. The sperm must compete to reach the egg, and being the winning sperm is important for survival. In feminine energy, there is only one. Once released from the ovary, there is only that egg that can create new life. No other. No competition. No comparison. When you date in feminine sovereignty, you are already the One.

In your feminine energy, you are like the egg. You are the All. You are the One. The masculine must seek to be the Best. The feminine is the One.

When you date as a feminine person, you are not in competition. You are not in competition with your date. Keep your eye out for a tendency to prove yourself to be intelligent, interesting, or worth dating. Watch out for instances where you create conflict in order to show that you are better than your date. There is no such competition.

You are also not in competition with other women or people your date might be interested in. You cannot compare yourself to other women your date has been with or may be with now. You are a singular event. Your connection with him is one-of-a-kind.

If there is another woman in the picture and that isn't what you signed up for, you are simply at the wrong dog and pony show. It doesn't mean he doesn't love you or care about you. It simply means he doesn't want what you want. You are not in a relationship to compete. When you worry about the competition, you are in masculine energy, and you will cloud up attraction with a man.

You are the One even if you consciously choose polyamory, meaning you don't set up the relationship dynamic to be this partner versus that partner or me versus my partner's other love. You are simply you. Uniquely and wholly connected to another person.

In feminine seduction, there is only you and your relationship with the Other.

No competition.

The Love I Wanted

My life in Copenhagen had a rhythm and flow to it, like a piece of music. I rode a baby blue cruiser bicycle through the city, ate amazing food prepared by my Bangladeshi roommates, and spent almost all day every day at the Vocal Institute learning and practicing songs and musical techniques. We had regular performances to showcase our work, one of these musical evenings being our Songwriter Concert. I was MC-ing the concert, and I was quite relaxed. I had spent the afternoon holding a baby who was the grandson of one of my classmates. For hours I had coo-ed at him and then cradled him as he fell into a deep sleep. It had been a long time since I'd held a baby, and I wasn't in a rush to give him up. He was there to watch his grandmother perform in the concert, so he stuck around all evening, learning to clap at each song. He also wanted to spend time with me up in front of the crowd.

Jesper was leading the band that accompanied the singers at the concert. He had long blonde curls and a face that resembled a mature cherub. His presence was gentle and kind. I had first noticed him nearly a year before when I attended a weekend workshop at the school, and he had been the piano accompanist for our singing then. He could listen to any song for a few minutes and then play it note for note. I had fallen fast in awe at his skill and in lust with his looks. But I had been dating Constantin at the time, so I reconciled the heat of my feelings as sex starvation. Jesper hadn't ever paid me any special attention, and I hadn't considered my attraction to him to be serious.

On this night, he paid attention to me, however. We communicated about all the songs, we fussed over the baby together, and I asked him a few emotional questions about his life. The next day, he sent me a Facebook friend request, and my heart jumped. He started a chat as soon as I accepted his request. He asked me if my cohort ever went out as a group. Incidentally, I had just organized a group evening out to a Latin dance club. I invited him to join us.

He showed up looking ready for dancing. He greeted everyone, but it was obvious he was there to see me. He placed his coat on the chair next to mine and asked me what kind of drink I'd like.

"A strawberry margarita," I responded, and off he went to get two.

We sat together, sipping our overly-sweetened margaritas and chatting.

"Should I teach you to dance?" I asked him halfway through our drinks.

"Sure," he replied. I felt he would have agreed to my suggestion even if I'd proposed a trip to Mars. I let him lead to the dance floor and then began to show him the steps of bachata. He grasped the rhythm quickly. Soon, we were dancing together, slowly and simply. Usually, I grew tired of dancing with beginners because of how few moves they know and how repetitive the dance becomes. Not with Jesper. I could have danced all night, but we took breaks to drink more and chat with some of my classmates. At the end of the night, only he and I remained.

We walked outside together, and he insisted on taking me to the train station on the back of his bike. I hadn't brought mine out. He set me on the back of his bike and wrapped his scarf around my neck.

"It's cold in the night air," he said, mounting his bike. We rode over to the central station, and he locked up his bike to walk me in. Something was wrong with my train pass, so he gave me an extra one he had. Accepting so much care, time, and energy was still relatively new for me, but I relished it instead of feeling guilty or overwhelmed as I previously would have. Saying goodbye and thank you, I tried to give his scarf back.

"You keep it for now," he insisted, "You need to protect your voice."

Our first date was at a small firelit coffee shop where I gave him back his scarf. I was supposed to meet a friend but got too wrapped up in our date. Realizing I was late, I told him I was sorry to go. He walked me out to the street, and we said our goodbyes. Then he leaned over and kissed me. I experienced a physical electric response. My body buzzed, and my mind went completely blank. Finally, exceedingly late, I got on my bike. I felt ecstatic as I pedaled through the damp streets of the Copenhagen spring. *Wheeeeee,* my mind cheered as the wind rushed around me.

On our third date, we walked along the canals of Copenhagen and then went back to his apartment to make out. I took a quick trip to Edinburgh, Scotland, to break up my EU travel visa time. He drove me to the airport and picked me up when I returned. He took me to an upscale seafood restaurant near the city waterfront on my birthday. We returned to his apartment and had the most loving, exciting sex I had ever experienced. For the first time, I had everything I wanted in love. I was in a loving, kind, thrilling relationship with an attractive, supportive, thoughtful man. He drove me to the seaside. He took me to the oldest amusement park in the world. Love was so easy. He wanted me around all the time, and I wanted to be with him all the time. My last month in the county, I lived almost exclusively at his house.

But the end of my program came, and I had to leave Denmark. Jesper drove my family (who had come to see my final performance) and me to Copenhagen airport. We had tentative plans to see each other in America that summer or in 90 days when my European travel visa reset. I was not anxious about these plans because I knew we would see each other again, one way or another. I traveled back to Istanbul for a visit and then on to my hometown of Portland, Oregon, to pay off vocal school and figure out my next steps in life.

I knew Jesper loved me. He had my picture as the background on his watch. In the end, he flew to America to see me. I took him on a road trip tour of America, just as I had previously done with tourists. On our road trip, things began to unwind. I was tired and stressed out, and he was tired and stressed out. When we were running out of gas during an 80-mile gas station-free stretch of mountains, he blamed me for not filling the tank. I was incensed. I wanted a partner, and here I was, being treated as someone's private tour guide. We fought and made up in Boise. The desert of Utah was stunning. I showed him one of my favorite places in Arizona, Horse Shoe Bend. He wasn't as impressed as I thought he might be.

We headed back toward the Grand Canyon and Las Vegas, and my car's air conditioning failed suddenly. My little Pacific Northwest car was unable to stand the desert heat. And now we couldn't either. Sweating and miserable, we rolled into a Honda dealership in St George to see what had caused our air conditioning failure. The repair would cost $1200, an expense I hadn't factored into our trip. But we couldn't keep driving in the desert with no air conditioning. He didn't offer to pay any of it nor support me well through my distress at this news. I was losing faith in him as my partner. I coughed up the money, and we were back on our way to the Grand Canyon, only now we had passed the South Rim of the canyon - where you can easily stop and see it from viewing points. Instead, we ended up at a big white tent where you could pay a good sum of money to be driven out to the Grand Canyon. Having already spent enough money that day and needing a break from Jesper, I sent him off alone with the canyon guide.

We arrived in Las Vegas late that night, and he wanted to party. I didn't feel like partying. He tried to guilt-trip me about this being his only time in Vegas. I found it hard to see that as the biggest issue presenting itself, but I rallied and went out with him so he could get some food, at least. I took him on a short sprint along the strip so he could see the main hotels, lights, and water shows. But my feet, back, and heart ached; I wasn't in a place to enjoy Vegas. We rounded off our trip with San Francisco, the Red Woods, and the Oregon Coast, arriving back in Portland exhausted.

When he left, I was no longer certain about our strong connection. I felt exhausted from spending so much time with him, instead of energized as I had in Denmark. We did not pass the travel test. I continued working through the summer and he and I continued chatting every day. Long distance was hard, and I slowly lost excitement about sexting him.

The day came to talk about our future if we were going to have one. I sat on the cement curb of a parking lot during a quick break from work. There were no convenient times to talk, with a nine-hour time difference between us. It came out that he didn't want to have children. I was flabbergasted. Somehow, I had taken it for granted that he would want children. We had first bonded over a baby, and I had somehow forgotten to clarify what he wanted in his future life. Five months of dating had slipped innocently by. I loved him, but I didn't love him more than myself or my future vision. This is when I learned the importance of letting men know what I deeply desire in life.

"Do you really not want children?" I asked him and caught my breath.

"No," he said, followed by a string of excuses.

"Oh," I said, defeatedly.

One more month, we hung on, no longer chatting every day. Our relationship seemed to thin out, like fabric fraying at the end. I was heading to Ireland, where he had planned to visit me at one point, but he didn't ask when my departure date was. I didn't bother to tell him. I flew back to Europe, and our chatting stopped.

Our connection was hot and heavy, but it couldn't withstand the reality of day-to-day life and the challenge of travel. In a way, our relationship was everything I thought I wanted. It was passionate, it was loving, it was light, and it was emotionally connected. I felt seen and cherished. I had remained true to myself most of the time during that relationship. I had been willing to stick up for myself. I had been able to compromise. I had ridden the chaos of my emotions during our road trip. But in the end, Jesper and I weren't heading down the same road of commitment and a deep and lasting family bond; to me, that made all the difference.

Exercise: Your Focus Creates Your Reality

The highest purpose of being sovereign in your energy is having a handle on your focus. Your focus determines your reality. To start, make a list of what's going right and what you're doing well in dating. Continue to focus on the things that go well.

Focus on who you are, not who you aren't.

Focus on what you are receiving, rather than judging yourself for what you aren't or haven't received in the past.

Focus on how your own body feels now.

Focus on the wildness inside you that wants to be expressed.

Focus on your own emotions.

Focus on being in timelessness.

Focus on getting into the process of relationship and connection.

I can almost guarantee that if dating is going poorly for you, you are focused on who you aren't, what you haven't got, how other bodies look from the outside compared to yours, how you could be better or more perfect, how other people feel instead of how you feel, how you can't seem to make your preferred romance timeline work, and how your love life should be instead of how it actually is right now.

Re-focus on your feminine being and make your next relationship choice from there. If you slip up and lose your energetic sovereignty at any point in the dating process, take a deep breath and re-focus on your feminine energy. Breathe and be. Breathe and be.

TL;DR

1. With all seven feminine energy shifts under your belt, you are ready to apply them in your dating life.

2. Using feminine energy principles will likely make you more attractive to all people, not just men you are dating.

3. Submissive and dominant don't apply in feminine, non-linear chaotic energy. There is no first and second in a feminine paradigm. The idea of submission only exists in a masculine paradigm. Leave ideas of domination and submission for bedroom games. Practice leading in your feminine energy on dates.

4. You are already The One for your perfect match(es).

5. Competition is not feminine energy. If you get the sense you are competing with other women or are often tempted to compete with your dates themselves, check yourself. You have slipped into masculine energy.

6. Comparing yourself to other women your date has been with or may be with now is a waste of energy. You are a singular event. Your connection with him is one-of-a-kind.

7. Your focus determines your reality. Focus on the positives of what's going right and what you're doing well. Focus on your being, receiving, your own body and emotions, wildness, timelessness, and getting into the process of dating.

CHAPTER 12

SEXUAL HEALING

If I had a genie in a bottle, I would wish that no person ever again be forced into or offer sex when she doesn't want it. I have never met a woman who did not have a hang-up about sex. Whether it was a past she regrets, sexual abuse still affecting how she shows up in life, outright fear of her own sexual journey, or simply body or age reservations, women struggle to feel whole in being sexual.

A large part of the mission of my feminine energy work is creating a world in which people who experience life as core feminine beings feel empowered around sex and their physical bodies. So, whatever you are holding onto energetically about sex, consider whether or how it affects your dating life.

Feminine Sexual Energy

You may have already gotten the inkling, and now I'll just say it - the concepts of feminine energy are based on the way females experience sex during the act of procreation. Additionally, broadly speaking, sex with lots of build-up and foreplay that is unconstrained by time, process-oriented rather than orgasm-driven, honors emotions, is body-centered, and has a raw and wild quality, is fulfilling for females. Timeless, process-oriented, emotional, physical, and wild. During the act of human procreation, the female role is to *receive* (the sperm) and then *be* (gestate life through her own existence).

That said, there are countless ways to have sex, and I purposefully don't give how-to advice on better sex because this book focuses on finding and nurturing your feminine seductress. While finding a compatible sexual partner is a huge part of dating, I do not advocate that you need to practice feminine energy during sex. I would never recommend shifting your authentic sexual needs or wants to match feminine energy principles—quite the opposite. To be clear, you don't need to practice feminine energy in bed in order to be a great seductress.

In fact, sex is a great place to experiment with your masculine energy: being highly active, giving pleasure, moving your focus around from physical to mental, from process to initiation, and getting excited about a time limit or orgasm goal. Sex is a perfect arena to switch masculine and feminine roles.

However, in the case that you *are* nervous about sex for any reason, be it past abuse, inexperience, or trust issues, I do recommend bringing feminine energy to bed - or wherever you're having sex - to support your being, body, and emotions.

Slow down.

Be. Notice how *you* are.

Experience your body.

Honor your emotions and your partner's emotions.

Receive your partner.

Focus on the process instead of orgasm.

Lose yourself in the timelessness of the moment.

Date Rape

(Trigger warning for those sensitive to abuse.)

A month after I met Max and many months before he took me to the sex club, I traveled alone to Milan, Italy. I took an eight-hour train and failed to bring food with me or find it along the way. As a result, I arrived at my hostel slightly shaking from hunger and unable to focus properly.

I dropped my belongings in my room and went downstairs to ask the receptionist where I could get food nearby.

"It's a bit far," he said.

"How do I get there?" I insisted.

"Actually, I'm off right now. I can show you," he said.

He grabbed his coat, and I followed him outside.

"We can take my car," he said, "it's faster."

I liked the word *faster.*

"I just need to do one thing," he said after we had been driving for five minutes.

I didn't protest as he pulled into the parking lot of an official-looking building. Although I was weak from low blood sugar, I followed him inside and down the halls of some bureaucratic office where he was delivering papers. The office workers eyed me suspiciously.

Finally, he brought me to a restaurant, an American buffet. "I'm hungry, too, I'll eat with you," he said, parking.

I was beyond caring whether he stayed or went. An American buffet meant all kinds of American food, like burgers and chicken strips, but most alluring was a table stacked full of fruit. I hadn't eaten pineapples, melons, or peaches for the entire year in Germany. I loaded my plate with fruit.

"Let me get you a drink," he said.

I drank what he offered, and the alcohol worked fast on an empty stomach that I filled with only fruit. I felt tipsy extraordinarily fast. I got the feeling that I didn't particularly like this man with me, but I was too polite to leave or ask him to leave.

I retrieved a plate of more solid food, and when I arrived back at the table, he had gotten me another drink.

"Oh, thank you," I said, though I didn't really mean it. I felt the other alcohol taking over my exhausted, calorie-starved system. I looked across the table at my dinner partner. His teeth were brown in some places. *Whatever you do, don't kiss him*, I thought to myself. And I finished my plate of food and drink.

The night moved into a browned-out blur that I have never truly remembered. We were at a casino. Or was it a bowling alley? Or both? I made out with him on the ball dispenser of the bowling alley. I won some money at the casino, and he lost it.

"Do you want to go hang out with my friends?" he asked.

"Yes," I must have said.

He pulled up to a hotel, and we went inside. His friend worked at reception and threw him a key. My memory started coming back online. We went up to a room with two twin beds by ourselves. He took his shirt off. I moved to the farthest away twin bed.

"Where's your friend?" I said.

"Oh, he works here," he answered, coming toward me.

"I can tell that. What are you doing?" I demanded as he tried to kiss me. He grabbed me and placed me on the bed, kissing me and caressing me. And then I got mad. I fought him. I pushed and shoved and elbowed. No, no, no, I repeated over and over and fought him like I meant business until finally, finally, he gave up and moved to the other bed.

I lost my favorite necklace that night but was not date raped.

Two years later, Elias, the man from my freshman German class, became single again after the year-long relationship he dumped me for. He texted me. I felt honored that a man with short-term memory issues remembered me. He was moving after graduation and wanted to know if I would help him pack.

I said, "Of course."

We did no packing, but we did make out, and I agreed to sleep over. I said, no sex. We made out some more in bed, and he tried to undress me. I said no sex. We made out some more while he tried to convince me to want sex, and I said no, thank you.

I was too tired by two in the morning to keep saying no. So I lay still, and he date-raped me.

In the morning, it was the same routine as when I dated him before. He didn't want to talk; he wanted me gone. He had things to do. I got in my car and drove away. I had had sex against my will. I couldn't answer my own inquiry of why I hadn't gotten in my car in the middle of the night and driven away from a man who didn't respect me.

A year after that, I worked a summer in Mexico, where protecting women is a common cultural practice. You don't leave women alone. Men are duty-bound to fend for and defend their women. Unfortunately, this unspoken vow of protecting women sometimes turns into a perception of ownership. I stuck with a large pack of friends when we went out. Near the end of my time, I was running short on friends, so one of the local guys took to walking me home after nights out. He was attractive, and rumor had it that he had an enormous penis. I wasn't interested enough in these two factors to want to date him, but I appreciated him looking out for me.

But then, one night, he accompanied me past the security gate and right up to my host family's apartment door. He kissed me, which I didn't mind until he took out his dick, as big as the rumors alleged, and shoved my face down to his member. *No!* I hissed out in the most forceful whisper I could muster while jerking my neck away. I did not want to wake up the neighbors or my host family with this scene. He was very insistent. Once again, I had to fight someone larger and stronger than me. The only advantage on my side was pure desperation and anger. I just had to distract him long enough to get my finger on the door. It opened via fingerprint. He tried to control my body while I did everything I could to avoid his control. Coins fell out of my purse, my lipstick smeared on the ground. My clothes were completely disheveled. I fought him down to the tiles and then stood up swiftly, placing my finger on the lock pad, slipping inside as it clicked open, and locking the door as quickly and quietly as possible.

In the morning, I sprang out of bed, praying my host mother hadn't opened the front door yet. I went to the entrance. My host mother was in the kitchen nook, frying up breakfast. I opened the door casually, trying to be inconspicuous. I gathered my coins and wiped up the lipstick smears.

"Borrachísima" - Super Drunk - said my host mother disapprovingly as I sat down to breakfast.

"Sí," I agreed with her, ashamed, rather than trying to explain in Spanish how the man who walked me home to keep me safe had violated me outside her door.

These stories affirmed my beliefs that *men only want me for sex, men are pigs when it comes to sex,* and *men are dangerous when they don't listen to you.* These are stories about men who believed they could take what they wanted. They believed what they wanted was more important than what I wanted, or perhaps they convinced themselves that I wanted them, too. They did not believe my *No.*

There are men like this in the world. Do what you need to do to learn to fight. Do what you need to do to decline drinks from strangers. Do what you need to do and leave in the middle of the night. Keep your masculine energy in your back pocket, ready to protect yourself when you sense physical danger. Be prepared to defend yourself if you place your trust incorrectly. You will find that when you are connected to your feminine energy, you are less likely to be attracted to men who don't take you seriously, don't listen to your words, and don't have your best interest at heart. Take care of you.

Sex and Dating

Hopefully, sex during dating for you looks a lot more like the sexy times I shared with Berk, Emil, and Jesper. I have exactly two rules to help you have this kind of exciting and fulfilling sex while dating:

1. Have sex when *you* really want to
2. Establish an emotional connection before sleeping together for the first time when you want the relationship to last.

Now, these two rules can contradict each other, which is why I also say to remember the paradox of wild energy. The rules are made to be broken. Simply be aware of the potential consequences of breaking the rules.

Potential Consequences

When you have sex even though you don't really want to, you may regret it: You will likely feel disempowered after. You may have agreed to sex because your strategizing mind told you it was the right time in the dating process, you thought he was hot, or you got tired of saying *no*, or you wanted to be liked. Unfortunately, having sex may not lead to the outcome your mind was secretly hoping for (that he would fall madly in love with you, be unable to resist you, want more of you and only you, for example). When you agree to sex without your full desire, it may not be great *because* you're not 100% into it.

When you have sex before you've established an emotional bond: You may be less comfortable voicing your sexual needs and wants, you may be less comfortable period, you may worry excessively about what he's thinking during and afterward, and you may worry or totally spin out when he doesn't text you immediately the next day. The sexual tension between the two of you may diminish (after all, it was resolved). You may find there is less to talk about after the sexual act, or there is less energy in the connection. Men are much more likely to leave your life after sex (they *won* the sexual chase). To be candid: without a sustainable emotional connection, the sexual connection better be hot as fire if you want him to stick around.

Of course, what if he's ridiculously attractive, and you really want to sleep with him now? I also say that's fine. Simply know the rules, and understand that you can create an emotional connection in less than an hour. There is no time requirement for emotional connection, which is why I don't teach 3-date or 6-month no-physicality dating. The emotional connection of a date is governed by quality, not the quantity of time spent together.

If you really like and want a man, focus on creating an emotional connection. Very often, beyond biological programming, what people are craving when they want sexual intimacy is emotional intimacy. Ask him emotional questions. The masculine wants to be invited into the feminine, meaning his emotional and physical world. He is likely secretly starving to be seen and honored for who he really is and to express himself and his masculinity fully, honestly, and powerfully. You are exactly the great seductress to encourage him to show up with his full emotional and sexual self.

Showing Up Powerfully After The First Time

Your first time or the day after you sleep with a new date for the first time can be an occasion of personal drama. Your mental chatter can go into overdrive. You may wonder if he really likes you, if he had a good time, if you'll ever see him again, whether you're better in bed than his ex, or where this relationship is going. You might even wonder about all of this at the same time. You may get lost in the messy chaos of emotion.

If that sounds like you, here is a bonus energetic distinction: Feminine fullness and masculine spaciousness. I found that remembering those energy differences helped me stay grounded in my power rather than spinning into the trauma space of abandonment and neglect after initial sexual contact.

The feminine wants to be filled, while the masculine craves space. After sex, this becomes heightened because you have both fulfilled your sexual desire. When a man doesn't text you right away the next day, even if your instinct is for fullness and contact, give him the honor of space. Absolutely text him that you had a great time if you did, and let him know whatever seems important to say. However, don't take that moment to suggest masculine structure by attempting to schedule another date the following weekend or ask him how he feels about exclusivity. Create space.

Please note that this is not at all to say *all men* require space *all the time after sex*. Simply be aware of the masculine energetic distinction and allow space for a new partner to get back to himself after you sleep together. *It does not mean he doesn't want you or that you aren't a priority if he doesn't communicate with you immediately after sex,* even if your brain tells you that.

Speaking Of Priorities... There's You

Just as it's a good practice to allow him space to get back to himself, make sure you reconnect to *yourself* after sex. Make *yourself* your top priority after having sex with someone new for the first time. What do you need to get you back to your own feminine being? Schedule fun activities with your friends. Meet up with coworkers. Take a yoga class. Have a traveling day. Have a Face-Your-Fears day where you sit with your mental chatter about dating and make friends with it. Be intentional about reconnecting to *yourself* after sex with a new date.

A masculine man who is serious about you will usually contact you quite quickly. However, if you're already in his space (texting, calling, or showing up at his house for example), he can't reach out to you. So, once again, double down on feminine energy.

Breathe. Focus on being you, notice what you are receiving from the rest of the world, be process-oriented (be here now, don't plan the next three months to 30 years with him). Slow down, practice experiencing and allowing your emotions without fixing them or acting on them, feel into the internal state of your body, and get into timelessness around when the committed relationship will happen for you. If you have established an emotional connection, he'll be back, probably quicker than your anxious or dismissive mind will allow you to believe.

Exercise: Make A Plan For Sexual Healing

If you do only one exercise from this entire book, let it be this one. Making a plan is healing in itself. Trauma, by definition, exists in areas of your life where you perceive you have unbalanced or no power. Your body and mind likely have learned this danger around sex. Making a plan to heal tells your mind that you do have power and acting on your plan tells your body that you are capable of caring for and protecting it. Reclaim your power and make a plan to heal.

1. To ground in your healing, write a couple of sentences about the objective of your healing. For example, *I want to heal my fear of sexual intimacy.* Or, *I want to heal my discomfort by speaking my truth about sex with men.* Then, write a few reasons why it's important that you heal your sexual Self.

    This can look like this: *When I'm healed, I'll experience sex in a whole new, exciting way. I won't be afraid of having a life partner because I'll feel grounded in our relationship and our sex life. Sexual healing will teach me so much about myself.* Or, something like, *Having a better grasp on the full spectrum of my sexuality and feeling less shame about it will help me experience more freedom and fun during sex and allow me to express myself more fully in life.*

2. Now, choose 3-6 healing modalities that appeal to you. Here is a non-exhaustive list of suggestions to get you started:

    a. Psychoanalysis

    b. Cognitive Behavioral Therapy

    c. Integrative Therapy

    d. Emotional Freedom Technique

    e. Coaching

    f. Pelvic Floor Therapy

    g. Hypnotherapy & Past Life Regression

    h. Transcranial Magnetic Stimulation

    i. Energy Healing

j. Sound Healing

k. Training in self-soothing

l. Art therapy

m. Dance

n. Self-expression

o. Journaling

p. Reading books

q. Meditation

r. Self Care

s. Travel/Change of scenery

t. Support groups

u. Friend group you trust

v. Sex toys/self-pleasure

3. Depending on your commitment to the healing you desire, you will want to choose a frequency for your healing activities. I recommend frequency over timelines for healing plans because healing is not linear and does not fit in a box. Instead, choose how often you will do the healing modalities you chose (this is a process-based goal, not a timeline-based goal).

   a. What do you commit to doing daily or weekly?

   b. What do you commit to doing monthly?

   c. Write it down, so you don't forget.

4. Then, answer these questions:

   a. What kinds of tools do you need to follow through on your plan? (calendar reminders, education, a journal, etc.)

   b. Who do you need to support you on your healing journey? Write down their names.

Remember, the way you think about sex today doesn't have to be the way you think about sex tomorrow. The relationship you have with sex right now doesn't have to be the one you have for the rest of your life. Send a signal to your brain that you have power and make a plan to begin healing your past. You and your greatest expression of intimate love are worth it.

TL;DR

1. Feminine energy is based on the way the female body experiences sex during consensual human procreation.

2. If you are nervous about sex for any reason, dive deep into your feminine energy during the experience: Slow down. Be. Experience your body. Honor your emotions and your partner's emotions. Receive your partner's body and receive pleasure from your partner. Focus on the process instead of orgasm. Lose yourself in the timelessness of the moment.

3. Remember these two rules: 1. Only have sex when you really want to, and, 2. If you want to date someone for a long time as well as a good time, wait until after you've established an emotional connection to have sex (remember that emotional connection is not time-bound).

4. You can totally break both of these rules; simply be aware of the potential consequences.

5. After the first time you have sex, or the first time you have sex with a new partner, create space for both of you to reconnect to yourselves as individuals.

6. Your mind may go into overdrive at the point of first sexual contact, but calm yourself by making yourself your top priority after sex. Intentionally schedule some activities that reconnect you to yourself.

7. If you do only one exercise from this entire book, let it be Making A Plan For Sexual Healing.

CHAPTER 13

COMMITMENT

My hope is that by this point in the teaching of feminine seduction, you are out in the dating field experiencing some major feminine energy magic. You can use the energy and seduction system in this book to create any kind of relationship you desire - including short-term. What you have read so far is all about the sexual energy that is necessary to cultivate attraction and sexual desire. At this point, you are armed with the knowledge and skills to go out and have as many hot and spicy love connections as you desire. This last chapter is about moving a relationship to a long-term or committed relationship *if that is what you want.*

Often, people feel that deep, committed love is *harder* to create than casual, short-term flings. I certainly did, and I created casual relationships over and over. Casual relationships are only easier if you are avoiding emotional connection. Adding emotional connection will ensure that a relationship is meaningful, and if what your date desires is also commitment, he will choose to commit to you. I spent most of my dating years saying yes to casual relationships because I did not say no to them. Remember that you always have a choice. You can begin today by being clear and strong about what you desire in love. You can decide to choose committed relationships from now on. I was able to move past the energy of casual by practicing emotional connection and saying no thanks to relationships that leaned casual.

The major difference between hot, short flings and lasting, committed relationships is that sexual energy does not always take center stage in the long term. Basically, you don't need to be seductive all the time. While the enlivened sexual connection and intentional emotional intimacy of seduction will support your long-term relationship, connection and sex drive change over time. The hormones involved in creating a sexual bond with another human don't usually last more than a couple of years. Additionally, in a long-term romantic relationship, there must be space for your own masculine energy, so you can accomplish big goals, create your home, go grocery shopping, raise children, and work on active, mental tasks with your partner. Remember that your masculine energy is an important part of you.

A committed relationship must be able to transition from the seduction phase to the bonded phase, where both partners are expressing their core sexual energy as well as the full spectrum of their masculine and feminine energy—doing and being—giving and receiving. Desiring and planning. Together and separately. None of this is to say you can't have a sexy and fulfilling match for years on end. That's my personal goal, and I must say, it's going well.

A healthy relationship can survive the transition from an attraction and sex-focused bond to a well-rounded partnership. A well-rounded partnership means there is space for your whole Self in the relationship, not just your seductive dating self. There must be room for your natural masculine and feminine energy, as well as your partner's masculine and feminine energy, in the connection. In a long-term relationship, there will almost certainly be times when you are the one giving and caretaking or the one taking charge of big actions or plans. In a strong bond, both partners are able to give and receive. Both partners feel safe and inspired to express emotion, physicality, and intellectual capacity.

In a healthy relationship, both partners feel seen, heard, loved, and wanted for their full energy.

How To Transition To Long-Term

If you are truly in your feminine sovereignty while dating, you will not feel pressure to nail down the relationship definition. You will go day by day, observing your date's behavior and attitude, connecting on deeper and deeper levels, and integrating more parts of your lives together. Because you are connected to your own being and well-being, you will be getting to know your partner from a place of ease and trust rather than fear and a need to control. There will be ease in scheduling time to see each other. There will be flow and flirtation when you are together. You will want to share more of yourself and your life with this person.

If you desire a specific level of commitment (marriage, exclusivity, etc.), voice it from your first date or on the dating app as part of your first impression. While you don't need to shove it in anyone's face, be clear and upfront about it. Again, this is why it's so important to be clear on your vision of love. If you don't know what you want, it's very difficult to communicate it, and you will likely appear weird energetically. That's how I used to date. "Yeah, we could be together or whatever. I don't know. Casual is fine until it isn't, you know? Let's just see what happens." This attitude did not inspire anyone to commit to me. You don't want to leave your date wondering what you want at any point. You want them focused on whether they want what you want and if they want it with you.

Once you meet someone hot and exciting who is interested in you and what you want, you're in business! It's time to keep that sweet seduction going, but it's also time to start introducing your masculine energy into the mix. You need your masculine energy, too, just like your body needs testosterone. You need masculine energy to get work done, to exercise your physical body, and sometimes to do things even when you don't feel like doing them. There is incredible value in masculine energy for the full gender spectrum. Your masculine energy is a powerful part of you, even as a sexually feminine being.

Introduce your masculine energy into the relationship *at an intentional pace*. Intentionally give your partner something and allow him to receive it, or initiate a date directly and observe his response. Lean into your feminine energy if he responds negatively or noncommittally. Take care of your feminine center. Remember, it is not your goal to control him or the connection. It is your goal to *be* in connection. Get curious about his response rather than being judgmental. Start to do things for him while being conscious of any tendencies you might have to mother or pander. Observe his capacity to receive. Allow him time and space with his emotions.

Be aware that conflicts can arise when masculine-feminine dynamics shift because it often makes things less sexy. Things that were sexy can become annoying. Behaviors that were cute can become unbearable. Your man may feel emasculated and withdraw, or perhaps you feel emotionally neglected and lash out. This is common and a byproduct of the fluid nature of energy. My intention is that in reading this book, you have become intimately acquainted with feminine energy, so now you can make an informed choice about whether to bring your masculine or feminine energy to any given situation. You can play with your energetic presence and responses.

The good news is that this transition will feel effortless if you have truly established a healthy and deep emotional connection with someone. While it may sound like a lot of brain work and even game-playing right now, when you are deeply connected to someone sexually and emotionally, transitioning your masculine energy into the connection will feel natural and easy.

Re-Seduction

Long-term relationships naturally have dips in sexual attraction and activity. So what to do when you're feeling like you want a little more spicy attention and action? Re-seduce your partner. At any point, you can re-ignite the sexual energy of your relationship by returning to the deep feminine energy state of seduction. I call this Re-Seduction. Return to seduction. Return to your sexual feminine energy self.

Before engaging your partner in energy play, do a quick self-assessment to check in on whether you've been aware of yourself, your physical body, your emotions, or timelessness and spaciousness lately. The sexual attraction is most likely to fizzle when you aren't tending to *yourself* in these areas. What can you do to give your own body, emotions, and well-being some extra love? Once you feel grounded in your feminine energy for yourself, bring your desires (for a date, connection, physical touch, sex, etc.) to your partner. Make an emotional request. Reconnecting to your feminine energy goes a long way in keeping a relationship sexy, alive, and thriving.

Last Ditch Dating

After Jesper, I swore off dating for a year. But a few months into that year, I suffered a vocal injury. The small musical career I was building with performances and meager but emotionally meaningful income came to a screeching halt. I couldn't sing and sometimes I couldn't even speak.

Suddenly, my primary purpose and passion in life were gone. Days turned to weeks, and I missed an audition. I had to cancel all shows and rehearsals. Regular doctors told me I simply had a lot of swelling and redness in my throat. The local voice doctor who would have looked down my throat at my vocal folds was booked out for three months. I felt uncertain and terrified about what was wrong with me and utterly powerless to heal myself. I didn't know what to do.

Feeling a loss of masculine purpose in my life, I decided to give myself the project of looking for a life partner. Using my usual dating app strategy, I found three matches, Robin, Arthur, and Grant. Robin turned out to be about 30 pounds heavier in real life than in any of his outdoorsy, highly active pictures. I found that speaking to him about his very indoor hobbies and goals, I couldn't recognize him from his profile. I felt almost catfished. We went out twice, but I could not bring myself to continue getting to know him. His initial deceit had broken trust before we'd even created it, and I sensed that he must have had a deep dissatisfaction or delusion about what he looked like now, which was a major turn-off. I could not recover a sense of excitement about him nor trust him enough to imagine a relationship with him.

Arthur was kind, funny, and comfortably nerdy to me. He wanted to get married. He was exactly the kind of man I wanted to be with, except for one thing. I wasn't sexually attracted to him. He had soft brown hair and twinkling eyes. He was good-looking and thoughtfully masculine, but for me, there was something missing from his presence. Knowing that sometimes sexual attraction can grow from emotional connection, I continued to date him for a couple of months. We went on walks along the city boardwalk, and he taught me to waltz. We had a picnic in the park, and then he began to invite me to his house. Once it became clear that he was ready to move our relationship to a sexual level and knowing in my own sovereignty that our match wasn't true for me, I could not continue to date him in good conscience.

The level of emotional intimacy we had meant to me that I needed to end things with him officially. I chose against doing a slow ghost, becoming too busy, or any of the myriad other techniques used to remove oneself from someone's life nowadays.

Becoming highly seductive and desirable has this one downside; very often, you will become the one who has to break things off with a connection, even if you've usually experienced things the other way around. It happened to me, and now it happens to my clients. When you are seductively feminine, people will want you and want to be near you and won't want to give you up. It will become your task to end a connection you're no longer interested in. There are ways to break up with grace and integrity, and this is the way I recommend.

How To Break Up When You're Not An Item

Breaking up when you haven't committed is an art form. Practice it as often as you need to, it does get easier with time, and your emotional honesty skills will improve as a bonus. Allow time for your feminine energy before and after the conversation. Here are things to keep in mind for your short-term dating break-up.

1. Make a plan for how to do it. Where will you be? What time of day is best? What medium is best to deliver your news? What exactly will you say?

2. Do it as soon as you're sure you want to end things. You will know in your body when that time is. Waiting makes things awkward (they're still texting you, you feel bad, and you may agree to something you don't want out of guilt and/or pity, etc.). Weird energy will be in the space, and you will suffer more the longer you wait.

3. Don't ghost. Even if you are the ghost, the other person can still be the one to haunt you.

4. A short and sweet text is okay for brief connections (one or two dates or phone calls). I recommend a phone call for deep emotional or sexual connections. On the phone rather than in person can feel safer for women (we sometimes have an outright or unconscious fear of being killed for standing up to or rejecting men). Acknowledge where you are and where your hesitancy and fears are coming from. Make a plan that honors where you are based on that awareness.

5. If you want or need to do it in person, choose a place with a level of privacy so the other person can process emotionally if they need to (i.e., in a house or at a quiet park rather than when they are out and about or have friends waiting for them.

6. Use direct "I" statements and be honest about the reason. Don't attempt a cliche like "it's not you; it's me." In the best-case scenario, leave the word "you" out of the equation and give a clear personal reason. "This isn't what I want long-term." "I'm unable to feel what I need to right now." "We have different values/goals/plans for the future, and I need to be serious about pursuing those now."

7. I have used the word "you" in variations of "you are great, but we are not compatible" when it came to sexual and emotional availability issues.

8. If appropriate, based on their reaction, acknowledge and express gratitude for them.

   a. "It's been great getting to know you."

   b. "I enjoyed spending this time with you."

   c. "You are really amazing, so thank you for this month."

9. Leave only as much openness for future contact as you truy want. When you are the dumper, do not say "we can still be friends."

10. Have a plan for your own emotional support after (girls' night out, a walk in the park, phone a friend or your mom). Even when you are the dumper and the break is a relief, you may not feel good.

Unless your current dating goal is to sample a large crowd - a valid and sometimes important strategy - may your last break up be very soon!

The Power of No

Grant was freshly divorced after his wife had cheated on him. We met for coffee in a hip and cozy coffee shop and found out how much we had in common. International experience, families in business, and growing up in the same town. He was handsome, intelligent, fun, and exactly the right amount of weird. He suffered from an undiagnosed illness that made his diet complex and strict. He lived his life with a masculine strength and discipline and an aura of sadness and depth that I found intoxicating.

I agreed to meet him at the farmers market for a second date. We walked around, and he bought fresh produce while I worked my feminine energy. We sat down for a coffee in a small cafe, and he began sharing some of his pain with me. I put my hands on his hands and felt his energy. I was just being with him. By the end of our time at the cafe, he was smiling widely.

We walked through a city park, and he asked me about the rings I was wearing, which were my parents' wedding rings. I thought they were the most beautiful rings ever created; they had been custom-made just for them. He then proceeded to tell me the story of his parent's marriage and their first kiss under the ashes of Mt. St. Helen's erupting. He stopped and turned toward me, bent down, and kissed me. There was an undeniable fire between us. When he pulled away, he looked triumphant.

"I wish you weren't busy tonight," he said.

"I'm not," I said, "I'm busy tomorrow night."

We had slightly miscommunicated during the planning of this second date. On the spot, he invited me over for a home-cooked dinner that night. I went over to his large and pristinely furnished house. I felt nervous in his presence as he chopped vegetables, and I had nothing to do but breathe deeply to keep my feminine center. I noted that I was *still* more comfortable doing than being. Grant had a habit of giving attention and then withdrawing it quickly. It kept me on my toes. I caught myself trying to prove that I was interesting and accomplished several times.

His cooking that night was delicious, and it was not lost on me from his lifestyle and habits that he was an excellent catch. We watched a movie that he chose, and I felt done watching it part way through. Instead of telling him that, I turned toward him, and we made out. I did tell him I wasn't ready for sex, so we allowed our physical touch to build tension instead of resolving it. I slept over, and he took me to brunch the next morning. In many ways, it was an actual perfect date.

That week, the COVID-19 pandemic began to sweep across the world. We had a date scheduled, but he began to feel sick, which made him nervous. It made me nervous that he might not want to see me again. I wavered on my feminine center. I went over to his house anyway and gave him an energy-healing treatment. He said he felt much better after and perked right up, but I felt depleted and unseen - which for me, are clear signs of over-giving. I spent the rest of the evening listening to him and attending to his thoughts. He did not ask much about me that day. He wasn't very curious about me.

Then the world shut down with the pandemic, and he disappeared. It hurt, but many parts of my life and the rest of the world were in upheaval. I was reminded that dating while dissatisfied with your life is more difficult. I had used dating as a crutch to soothe my emotional pain, and it hadn't felt powerful.

Then Grant came back with a text. He apologized and said it wasn't like him to ghost, but things had been difficult for him due to the pandemic. It was a once-in-a-lifetime global crisis, and I decided to give him another chance. When the initial shock of the pandemic wore off, we went hiking in the open air, flirting our way through the woods. He kissed me again, which at a time of Covid contagion uncertainty felt highly forbidden, scandalous, and erotic. By touching lips, we had entered a pact of pathogens together. I agreed to another dinner at his house.

I went to his house intending to sleep with him. We walked around his neighborhood, and he talked about how much he loved his house and living there. I tried not to drown in misery at the not-quite-there-yet state of my life. My career, home, and dream life all felt far beyond my reach. My voice had still not healed, and I was spending most of my free time alone in silence. Speaking hurt, so singing was still out of the question, and I had stopped listening to music because it was too hard for me not to sing along.

As we returned to his house, he made an offhand comment about his ex that was bitter rather than bearing the flavor of I-have-moved-on-and-I-am-now-capable-of-trust-again. I knew I should be careful and go even slower with a divorced man, but I wanted him so much. It had, once again, been over a year since I had slept with a man, and he and I had built up lots of unresolved sexual tension over five months.

He began slowly, touching me gently. I wanted him so much I surrendered quickly. We moved to the bedroom, and he looked for a condom. He couldn't seem to find one and got quite verbally aggressive. I shrank back into my shell. But finally, he found one, and penetrational sex was back on the table. We had it, but I felt disengaged. He asked for a blowjob, and I delivered. He cheered me on, and even though my jaw hurt and my back ached, I did not stop pleasuring him until he came. He lay down, once again relaxed and energetic. I lay down next to him and waited. I assumed that it was now my turn to receive pleasure.

We talked instead. I was patient in case he was just recovering sexually. He did accents, and I laughed. The hours passed. My turn did not show up. Finally, midnight came around and he announced that he had to sleep and motioned for me to leave. I was not sleeping over this night. I was crushed. In a way, I had never been so humiliated in my life. The sexual experience felt more humiliating than when I had been date raped because I had behaved against my will so complicitly. Then he kicked me out of his home in the middle of the night. I had never had another man do that in my entire miserable dating history. I drove home feeling shaken and dirty.

This wasn't supposed to happen to me. I was a dating expert. I actively practiced healthy dating. I had written the course on the sexual energy of seduction. I knew all about dating success, holding my composure, honoring my own body and needs, not over-giving, and creating honest emotional connection. I had studied and practiced, and experienced incredible relationship success. And still, I had shrunk myself down into a scared ball with something to prove to a man, and I had failed to communicate my needs in connection and in bed.

It is easy for me to expect perfection from myself; in that case, I expected myself to practice feminine energy dating perfectly. The next day, I walked alone in my local park at dusk, reflective and full of grief. Finally, I found a grassy corner of the park where I could sob into the gathering darkness. I did just that. How could I let this happen to me? I lay down on the earth and let go, totally surrendering to the emotional pain, the physical humiliation, and the chaos of my thoughts. I cried and cried, wiping my runny nose with my hand and then onto the grass. How could I know all these strategies to create healthy relationships and still not use them? I was beside myself.

I noted how I had started my dating search in quiet desperation, with the pain of losing my voice, the uncertainty I felt about what I was supposed to do with my life if I couldn't sing, and using dating as a distraction. I noted how most of my time with Grant was about his preferences, his neighborhood, his farmers market shopping, his home, his cooking, and his taste in movies. I saw that I had liked the fantasy of fitting into his life because I didn't have the roots of my own life holding my center yet. I had only moved back to the country three months before meeting him. I needed to forgive myself for being scattered and unsettled.

After an hour of sitting in the dark field, I broke up with him via text, citing "incompatibility." He immediately agreed to our break. Instead of just imagining that he didn't care about me, I imagined that he suffered from the relationship trauma of sexual betrayal and that his unreadiness to treat me well sexually was not at all related to me. I had to dig deep to process that our break didn't mean I was unlovable, foolish, or worthless. There was immense power in my no thank you to continue our connection. That *no* created a new self-trust in me. That *no* proved that I was ready to take care of myself above the feelings of the men I wanted. That *no* meant that I was ready for commitment because I was finally ready to accept nothing less.

If learning no is important for you, and committing to yourself and your vision before others is not your first instinct, you will likely face a similar lesson. Take care of yourself and say *no* to anyone you need to. You must be able to say *no* to anyone who cannot or does not want to engage in the kind of relationship you want. You must be able to say *no* to a love that doesn't match your standards, needs, or desires in order to signal to your brain that you want something different. *No* is a tool to create space for the love you really want. *No* is a prerequisite for a wholehearted yes later on. You will need *no* to get to happily ever after.

Happily Ever After

Much of the scientific research I conducted during my study of love was to answer the simple question, how do you create a happy commitment that lasts? As a child of divorce six times over - my own parents, their subsequent partners, and all but one of the host families that housed me in various countries at some point in my early life, I was no stranger to the end of love and commitment. I was very concerned with the phenomenon of relationships ending before I even had intimate relationships of my own. What was the cause of all this relationship and family destruction? How could I prevent my own relationship from going this way? What makes a relationship last? Many books are devoted to this subject, and I invite you to dive into what other experts and authors say. Some of my personal favorites are Esther Perel, Helen Fisher, and John Gottman.

It's important to note that the world has changed since the dawn of human procreation, and societal rules have changed rapidly in the past one hundred years. We no longer rely on the support of a small tribe to gather food, build shelter, and collectively work toward the continuation of human life, AND many of us are moving beyond the societal requirement of monogamous marriage for women to control paternity. The time of female fulfillment beyond servitude to the family is coming. You don't need to choose the dating end goal of long-term commitment.

You may not want a *forever* relationship. You may not like the structure of marriage. You may want something other than a family. You may not want to commit to anyone at all, ever! It is totally your choice. I wanted the structure of marriage for legal reasons (taxes, children, hospital rights) and emotional reasons. For me, the commitment of marriage facilitates a space of deep trust and partnership where I can unravel my own traumas, triggers, and ability to connect and be intimate. I wanted to be alongside a man who committed to me at the level of intending *till death do us part*. I wanted to be with someone who declared our union of love and future to people and state and who wanted to intertwine our lives and DNA.

After Grant, I quit all dating apps and continued chatting only Berk. We sexted, and he sent me memes, music, and TV show recommendations. His messages made me blush with my entire body, and sometimes he made me laugh out loud. But halfway across the world and stuck in his own pandemic-sized emotional hole, he could not provide the kind of emotional and physical intimacy I deeply desired. I began to get the sense that I was once again waiting for a man who hadn't promised me anything. I wanted him to offer to visit me or to invite me to see him, but the invitation didn't come. The sexting was enlivening, but I wanted something with more emotional depth. I realized that Berk still represented my old pattern of holding out for something that hadn't been offered.

As I got ready to launch my signature group program, *The Art of Feminine Seduction*, I committed to practicing what I preach and going on feminine seduction dates. If I was going to champion women dating for better relationships, I needed to be on the path I endorsed. I needed to practice dating. So I got on a new dating app and sent a few messages. I was uninspired by the responses I received, but I relished the masculine attention and kept going. One unsuspecting Thursday evening, I was swiping through profiles before I went out to meet a friend at a neighborhood patio bar. I glanced over the profile of a highly attractive man claiming he was looking for "someone who enjoys deep conversations over nachos and who is into personal growth." *Well, that's exactly me,* I thought and messaged him that I was a big fan of nachos, deep conversations, and personal growth.

While I sat at the bar with my friend laughing over cucumber gin and tonics, he wrote back asking me if I wanted to grab nachos the next day. I had absolutely nothing to lose, and I trusted that in this dating round, I would stay connected to myself and get out of there as soon as something felt off. I said I would love to meet.

That Friday night was my first date with my husband. I had no agenda beyond making a connection. I dressed as my favorite version of myself and was well-rested and hydrated. I was emotionally ready to get to know another person. From our first encounter, I noticed he had an incredibly rich and resonant voice, he was confident but humble, he spoke with integrity, he was intelligent and interesting, and he was *interested* in who I was and what I thought. Besides being incredibly handsome, he was genuinely likable right from the first encounter.

We broke several traditional rules of great first dates. We lingered for 6 hours, we shared stories of our exes, and I ate very few nachos and drank two ciders too quickly. The sugary alcohol caused me to feel fuzzy-brained and unable to drive home safely. He walked me around the neighborhood, trying to help me sober up. I was leaving town early the next morning and did not want to deal with retrieving my car from that side of the city. He happened to live within walking distance and offered to let me spend the night. I agreed to stay at his place on the condition that there would be no sex. He was an absolute gentleman. I fell asleep in his arms. Before drifting off to sleep, my last thought was how perfectly our bodies fit together.

The next few weeks rolled into months. We formed a quick but deep friendship. Though work sometimes took us apart, we spent most days and all evenings together, curled up on the small gray couch in his apartment or holding hands on long walks in the winter dark. He learned to make eggs benedict, the meal I always ordered at brunch, and then made them for me every morning. I did not worry about his feelings for me. He spoke of his care and demonstrated it in his actions. I was more honest with him than I had ever been with a man before. I allowed him to listen to my side of phone calls with friends and family, something I had never allowed anyone to do previously. I did not experience anxiety about where the match was going. I was fully in the moment with him, enjoying his company, personality, idiosyncrasies, and affection for me.

I cannot exaggerate how effortless the connection was and how naturally the decision to commit came. We both wanted the same kind of relationship. We both genuinely admired each other and treated each other with love and respect at all times throughout our courtship.

He asked me what I would think about marrying him three months into the relationship. When a man falls in love, he may not take long to decide you are the one. Masculine energy is direct and purposeful. Once again, feeling into the emotional and physical safety I experienced in my body around him and his question, I replied that I would say *yes* if he asked me. Several months, conversations, ring trials, and a road trip later, he asked me to marry him on a sunny April day in a charming vacation town nestled in the Cascade mountains. Though several parts of our relationship moved fast, the energy was never hurried. Fast is fine, but rushing can be a trauma response rather than an aligned action. I was not in a rush to get to commitment. I was not in a rush to get to marriage. I wanted those things but I went into them without a sense of urgency—pace matters.

Our relationship has continued to morph and flow. We have added layers of meaning to our initial commitment by moving in together, introducing each other to larger and larger circles of family and friends, getting married, and combining our futures. In the private corners of our relationship, we grow individually, and as partners, we deepen our trust, our knowledge of the other, and our ways of being together and apart. I continue to date my husband. It is my personal goal to date him for the rest of my life. I continue to be curious about what he loves, who he is, and who he is becoming. I re-seduce him as often as I can, preferably every day. I keep my commitment to my vision of an intimate and passionate partnership.

Creating a committed relationship can become simple if you have done the energy work in this book and you are fully connected to yourself and what you want. Finding commitment is only tricky if you're uncertain about what you want or if you're trying to force a relationship on someone who doesn't want to commit. Happily ever after is closer than you think.

Not Forever

But here's the thing: nothing is forever. The juicy hormonal state of seduction does not last forever. When you fall in love, your body floods with the love potion of relationship creation: dopamine, oxytocin, norepinephrine, etc. Studies estimate that your hormone levels stabilize between 1.5 - 2 years into your relationship and return you to your pre-in-love state. People usually experience this period of romance as a falling out of sexual desire or at least a diminishing sexual desire for their partner.

Esther Perel asks the great question, can you want something you already have? Her query characterizes the two-year mark in a committed relationship. If you are solidly bonded to each other, do you still want each other? This point in a bond is when you become more prone to fighting because your primal urge for sex with your person is chemically fading, while your emotional attachment to them has usually become stronger. This means that your partner's approval, validation, and desire for you can become what feels like a matter of life and death, while your desire for passionate physical connection is simultaneously diminishing. Basically, you get less sexy vibes and more threats to emotional survival. You will no longer be consistently floating on cloud nine-level love. One of you may stop saying yes to make the other person happy. Both of you will spend less time feeling enamored with the other and more time dealing with your emotional baggage together. This is the time when most relationships end.

If your goal is to get through this stage, remember Tuckman's Stages of Group Development: Forming, Storming, Norming, and Performing. This point in an intimate relationship is the Storming - becoming angry, upset, and stormy with your partner. Just remember, it is a natural part of creating a relationship. The way you repair after hurt and conflict is where you will see the growth and development of yourself and the partnership. As you practice being with the feminine energy of wildness and the unknown, conflict will begin to feel less dangerous. The *not-forever* nature of the world will feel less threatening. You will gain a greater capacity to see the shades of gray in the relationship between your partner's bad behavior as opposed to your own virtuous behavior. In positive and healthy relationships, the conflict will help you grow rather than tear you down.

Conflict is normal, necessary, and can even be healthy as long as you repair in a way that is satisfactory for both parties. Get the support of a Marriage and Family Therapist, Counselor, or Relationship Coach if the way you repair is unhealthy. Keep in mind that a relationship with someone unable or unwilling to repair with you reliably is unsustainable.

It's normal to sometimes feel lost, confused, lonely, or misunderstood in long-term relationships. That is a condition of having a human mind and attempting a deep and lasting connection between a separate person and yourself. Be wary of sticking around in relationships where feelings of confusion or loneliness are the norm. However, in positive and healthy connections with good repair habits, know that there is a norming and performing light at the end of those feelings. Feelings aren't forever, either.

Forever is a state of carrying on rather than constantly feeling, being, or experiencing the same rush of new love energy. However, I always recommend returning to the excitement of a new relationship through your feminine energy. Continue to date your long-term partner. Re-seduce your lover as often as you want. Know that it may take a few storms to create a real relationship rainbow. A healthy storm isn't forever, either.

How To Practice Feminine Seduction

You are now an Initiate into the power of Feminine Seduction. You hold the keys to your sexual power in your hands. The kingdom of emotionally and sexually fulfilling love is yours. Are you applying what you learned in this book? Are you practicing the energetic shifts? You do not need to be an immediate energy master to become a great seductress. Begin with one step.

Applying these energetic shifts all over your life will begin to shift things in ways you probably can't even imagine right now. You will become more lit up, more attractive, and more seductive, all in perfect time. Like my own story, love may not come to you in one day, after one date, even if you are practicing with the level of devotion I did. And then again, it might. Just don't give up if your ideal love match doesn't come knocking right away. Continue to practice becoming aware of your energy and shifting when necessary. Get into the process. Shift your energy one juicy feminine practice at a time. Be leisurely and luxurious about learning seduction. No need to perfect anything by tomorrow. Remember that slow is sexy and that slow change is sustainable.

There is a great seductress inside you, and I can't predict what the process of your uncovering, healing, and honoring her will look like. I can only promise that the journey will be worth it. The best time to start practicing is before you are ready. Take what you have learned from past relationships and from this book, and use what you love. Toss out anything that doesn't match your needs, style, or heart's desire.

When you need outside support along your dating journey, ask for it. Learning to accept support is a vital step in becoming a great seductress and being part of a relationship that lights you up and makes you feel seen and supported.

If love is what you want, declare it. When you tap into and acknowledge what you want and then make moves to create it, you are an embodiment of the sacred masculine-feminine dynamic. Feel what you want and act on it. Practice creating the love you want to have in that simple action. Any of the shifts outlined in this book can be easier said than done. It can be difficult to rewrite a lifetime of feeling validated for doing rather than your being, for giving rather than receiving, for your intellect rather than your emotional capacity, and for relying on accomplishments to prove how worthwhile and lovable you are. If you are more comfortable starting to accept support outside the context of dating, I and countless other dating coaches and therapists are out there waiting to serve you. Your next step might be reaching out to someone who can support you through a feminine energy embodiment process beyond what a book can offer. There is no one path to reclaiming your sexual power, but it is always a worthwhile path to travel.

While the promise of how dating can be using the shifts and techniques outlined in this book may seem far out of reach today, all you need to do today is take one step. Observe one major energetic tendency you have (mine is a proclivity for doing over being), and acknowledge one way in which dating currently isn't working for you. So much can unravel and shift from that simple practice.

Since you read all the way to the end of this book, I know one thing for sure: you are committed to the path of love, and that means you are already on that path right now. Being on the path is a neon sign that your partner is somewhere down the same trail, heading toward you. So take one step toward them.

Your journey as a great seductress is seven energy shifts away and each shift is available right now.

TL;DR

1. The key to the energy of a long-term relationship is to integrate your sexual energy and your on-the-go energy, so you can express both feminine and masculine as often as you like.

2. Introduce your masculine energy into the relationship *at an intentional pace.*

3. Re-seduction is the name I gave to returning to deep feminine energy and the seduction tools from the beginning of a relationship: creating attraction, sexual tension, and an emotional connection. At any point in the relationship, including when you are in the middle of building a shed together or after having children, you can recreate this sexy energy in your love life.

4. Becoming highly seductive and desirable has one downside; very often, you will become the one who has to break things off with a connection, even if you've usually experienced things the other way around.

5. I highly recommend learning to break up effectively with someone you're not committed to in order to keep your dating energy clean and prove to yourself that you will stand up for what you want.

6. You must be able to say *no* to a love that doesn't match your standards, needs, or desires in order to signal to your brain that you want something different.

7. Nothing is forever, but that also means that tough spots in a relationship aren't forever either, if both parties are committed to getting through the storm.

8. When it comes to feminine seduction, practice makes perfect. So start practicing today, and reach out for support if you need it.

ABOUT THE AUTHOR

Alana was always a strong independent woman who didn't need a man, but the thing was - she really wanted one.

She searched high and low, in multiple workplaces, through several educational institutions, and on three different continents. All she found were bad date stories, an accidental kidnapping, and the sincere belief that she was a failure in love.

In an effort to fix herself, she dove into mating, dating, and connection research. She consumed every book, podcast, TedTalk, YouTube video, article, and course that came her way from top marriage therapists and dating experts. She began to see common threads in all of them, leading her to create the concept of Feminine Seduction.

She applied the concept to her own dating life and things began to turn around immediately. She was asked on more dates, had more effortless fun while dating, and created meaningful connections with men who made her feel special and desirable. Eventually, she also found The One she was looking for.

As a bonus, she found a life path as a teacher and Dating Coach, empowering women to connect with their own seductive allure in order to create the love they want.

Alana lives in Portland, Oregon with her husband and a jungle of houseplants. She spends her time studying and teaching relationship skills and vocal technique. She enjoys singing, playing piano, and composing music, as well as spa treatments, reading, and being near bodies of water.

Alana runs a number of ongoing workshops and transformational retreats. You can learn more about her and how to work with her at sovereign-dating.com.

You can also find and follow her on

Youtube: youtube.com/@sovereigndating/featured
Instagram: instagram.com/sovereigndating/
Facebook: facebook.com/sovereigndating/
LinkedIn: linkedin.com/company/sovereign-dating-coaching/

BOOK CLUB QUESTIONS

1. What was your favorite dating story in the book and what did you learn from it?

2. Which of the three seduction ingredients is most challenging for you (Attraction, Sexual Tension, Emotional Connection)?

3. Did reading the book impact your mood? If yes, describe how so?

4. What aspects of the author's story could you most relate to and why? How did that make you feel?

5. What did you already know about feminine energy dating before you read this book?

6. What new things did you learn about feminine energy dating?

7. Which of the seven feminine energy shifts feels most relevant to your life?

8. Describe three significant ah-ha's you had after reading this book.

9. Describe three places where you got triggered.

10. What was your biggest takeaway from the book?

www.ingramcontent.com/pod-product-compliance
Lightning Source LLC
Chambersburg PA
CBHW052016030426
42335CB00026B/3164